Learning

Master the Science of Accelerated Learning to Read Faster, Memorize More and Master Anything With Ease

(Study Skills to Boost Your Gpa)

Colin Smith

Published by Rob Miles

© **Colin Smith**

All Rights Reserved

Self Learning: Master the Science of Accelerated Learning to Read Faster, Memorize More and Master Anything With Ease (Study Skills to Boost Your Gpa)

ISBN 978-1-7771171-6-0

Legal & Disclaimer

The information contained in this book is not designed to replace or take the place of any form of medicine or professional medical advice. The information in this book has been provided for educational and entertainment purposes only.

The information contained in this book has been compiled from sources deemed reliable, and it is accurate to the best of the Author's knowledge; however, the Author cannot guarantee its accuracy and validity and cannot be held liable for any errors or omissions. Changes are periodically made to this book. You must consult your doctor or get professional medical advice before using any of the suggested remedies, techniques, or information in this book.

Table of Contents

Introduction

One of the fundamental values of every human being is the set of skills and knowledge available to solve problems. The only way to get this set is learning. The value of learning has as its purpose the habitual search for knowledge through study, reflection of lived experiences and a deep vision of reality.

Our life is surrounded by many situations around our daily work, family and personal relationships of all kinds, in each place we must take initiatives, solve situations and teach others to work, create a better coexistence and lead a better life . Whoever has more elements within his reach, is able to fulfill this task effectively, because this value does not consist in accumulating knowledge to be a scholar, but to serve. There are those who since the time of students have believed that we should only learn what is necessary and indispensable to perform a specific professional work, worse, that there is no choice but to make the minimum effort to solve an academic situation. But why does it make us lazy to learn? Simply because we want everything to have practical and immediate usefulness (like the child who learns to count and to know the denomination of the coins, to buy with the security of not being deceived); This without adding the effort and time involved in being in front of a book or any other medium. What a lack of aspirations and wishes for self-improvement! Occasionally we find people with the ability to draw conclusions almost instantaneously, having a response and explanation for any matter, anyway, as if they knew everything; The astonishment is greater if it is a cardiologist opining about public administration and refers to the history of any nation ... Without detracting from personal skills, the exceptional - and product of learning - is

2

the ability to relate facts, knowledge and Experiences to have a well-formed criterion and give a timely and accurate response in each case. We must not forget that personal development involves professional improvement, therefore, we must be concerned to deepen. Finishing college, starting a master's degree, undertaking a doctorate, attending refresher courses and graduates should be a natural path. We can not forget that in today's working world having a university degree is no longer enough. It is necessary to go further if real progress is desired. However, there are other areas that apparently are not directly related to our work: history, philosophy, doctrine, literature, human relations; Or technical and scientific knowledge: program management for computers (computers), business administration, human body functioning, first aid, notions of automotive mechanics or any manual dexterity. Getting additional knowledge to our profession or trade will always be of practical use and will give us a broader picture of life.

In a way it could be said that everything begins as a hobby, that learns by itself enjoys the activity without questioning when and for what will serve the subject in question, and it is becoming easier to learn, because like the body Human, the intellect also needs to develop.

When we are not human and professionally prepared, we are unable to prevent and solve problems: if a parent does not notice the training that his children receive in school, he will find no explanation for his behavior changes; Having a company leaving the administration in the hands of others, is not always convenient; Managing personnel without having basic notions of behavior and human nature, leads to impersonal treatment; Disregarding the dignity of marriage and family, may result in disintegration.

Faced with our inability, we become dependent on circumstances and people, seeking guilty and avoiding responsibilities. A person in constant preparation, is interested in everything that surrounds his peers because he wants to overcome himself and find a way to be more useful. We must accept that we do not fully understand many of the current events, much less notice the repercussions they have for our society and the family in particular: why customs have changed so much in the last 50 years; Why we now talk about quality and leadership; Understand current controversies over human life; International conflicts. We could fill with examples and the concussion would be the same: it is necessary to learn more to understand better what happens in our life and in the world, to stop thinking that everything is a chance or a product of the efforts of a few. To grow in this value, we need to keep in mind that learning something new is not a waste of time, it is a way to achieve self-improvement. We could argue lack of time and need for rest, but everything is a matter of organization and effort, perhaps in a gradual but continuous way.

To reinforce the value of learning you can:

Make it a habit to read at least one book per month.

· Finish college (if you have not already done so)

· Sign up for an update course or a graduate

· Begin mastery

· To obtain a doctorate

· Listen to newsletters, read the newspaper and approach media that provide information about the reality that surrounds you.

· Buy magazines on topics that are additional to your profession or trade

· Look carefully at the attitudes of others and seek conclusions that will serve you in the future.

· Develop a new hobby that allows you to gain new knowledge in an area you do not know.

The value of learning makes us people who have more tools to advance in life and to be better human beings.

Chapter 1: What is Accelerated Learning?

Many of us remember sitting in a classroom or training center at one time or another feeling completely lost. The teacher ends the session and asks if there are any questions. You feel as if you should raise your hand and ask if she or he can simply go over everything just one more time.

But why does that happen to us? For many, it happens more frequently than we are willing to admit. In large part, this occurs because the teaching method employed is not adaptable to the way we ourselves learn. Therefore, we spend a great deal of time taking information and attempting to translate it into a method we understand before we can even begin the task of processing the data and applying it.

Researchers have found, however, that human actually used some consistent methods to learn and analyze information.

Consider them the natural reflexes of our brains. By tapping into these natural learning methods, researches have been able to create a means of increasing the speed and retention of students, employees and those within the management of any specific industry.

The reason that accelerated learning appears to be so successful is that it does not just involve one part of the body or one area of the brain. This method is all encompassing, involving creativity, physical activity, images and even music to help an individual drill down into their deeper learning potential. Individuals find themselves deeply drawn into the learning process, thus making what they are learning stick with them even better.

Yet to really get the most out of this type of learning method, one needs to have the type of environment that is conducive to accelerated learning. What is involved in the optimal environment? First and most important, the learning environment needs to be positive, providing the students with a can do feeling. If students feel stressed, unsafe or a lack of interest in the material, they will not truly benefit from the other areas of the learning method.

What are some ways to create this positive learning environment? Consider adding a stretching exercise or deep breathing to the beginning of a learning session to give students a chance to release their stress from the day prior to diving into the material. If the material is work related, it is important to inform your students early in the session about how they can personally benefit from the data being covered. This will allow you to peak their interest in the material. Creating interest for your students might vary depending on your audience and the material that is to be covered during the accelerated learning session.

Where are you holding the session itself? This will come into play if the area is considered unsafe. When students are concerned about their own safety or protecting their belongings, such as a purse or car, an instructor is not going to have their full attention. Optimal accelerated learning is not likely to take place as a result.

When an instructor takes in the emotional, physical and social environment of her students, she can find ways to tweak the learning environment to reflect a more positive student experience. Students who feel positive and invigorated to learn are now ready to maximize their own natural learning abilities to absorb these new skills or data.

By creating this type of learning environment, an instructor is attempting to engage the total student. Passive learning means that the student is not necessarily active in the process. Imagine a situation where you are just observing the actions of others without participating in the process. We can take a baking lesson as an example. While you might pick up some of the techniques involved in creating that beautiful cake or dessert, those who are able to participate in the process find themselves retaining more knowledge and gaining valuable experience.

Accelerated learning works on a similar ideal. Students are involved in the learning process, using activities that get them moving and thinking. Thus, presentation or material based learning experiences are typically avoided, because they can be less engaging for the students.

As our baking example also showcased, the best learning experiences are often a collaborative effort. Social interactions through group activities can assist in engaging those students who might otherwise be turned off due to a lack of interest in the topic or skill set to be mastered. When creating any lesson plan with accelerated learning at its core, it is critical to make sure the students are engaging, not only with the instructor, but with the other students. Learning collaboration involves the students with their instructor, but also with their fellow learners. Each individual student benefits from the strengths of the others as they take on a new skill set.

Another social aspect is the understanding that each individual has their own particular learning style. Often the variety of learning options, in terms of activities, can engage all of your students to their fullest levels. Instead of a one size fits all approach, accelerate learning focuses on creating a learner centered approach that encourages all students to engage their five senses completely.

With our baking example, our five senses play a key role in achieving the best results in terms of the final product. It would be improbable to create an amazing dessert if you cannot taste it, smell it or were unable to confirm that you were using the proper ingredients from sight. In much the same way, a learning experience needs to immerse a student's five sense in the material. The results should drive the choice of learning method, versus the learning methods driving the results. Accelerated learning is based on choosing the methods that work for a student to achieve their desired results.

So what type of results can drive the choosing of a learning method? Results might include the learning of a new and detailed skill set. Those in the skilled trades often use the learning method of encouraging their students to be hands on with both their tools and materials. As they practice together and under their instructor's watchful eye, they find themselves immersed completely in the material. The students are also benefitting from the experiences of their fellow students, thus contributing to a rich learning environment for everyone. It is easy to see how these skills can be mastered as students work diligently in a social and immersive environment.

This example leads to the importance of context in terms of learning. In the skilled trades, one has to understand how to use a tool in the proper context, building on their knowledge from tool to tool. Thus, their skill set continues to grow as one learning experience builds on another. Does this mean that facts by themselves are not important within the learning process? No, various pieces of data are necessary, even in a single fashion. Yet, accelerated learning focuses on creating context to the material. By doing so, the material is easier for the students to retain, because they understand how it relates to other aspects of the information. However, learning is a continual process. It involves immersing oneself in the material, then accepting feedback, reflecting and evaluating the results, then reimmersing one back into the education process. Accelerated learning promotes a complete immersion in the education process as critical to success.

Most students who have used this type of method to learn a new skill or a set of facts for a specific project or position find that they are able to retain more. Therefore, they are better able to execute their newly acquired skill set, as well as add to their knowledge through continual practice.

So what are a few of the techniques that can have learners helping themselves and each other? One such method is called the collaborative review circle. The class of students stands in a circle. Each student is provided a double-sided card with green on one side, but red on the other. When the students are questioned about a method or fact, those that believe they have the answer should flip their cards to green.

Those who do not know are meant to flip their cards to red. Those with the red card must find the answer by reaching out to one of the students who has a green card. Afterward, the instructor reveals the answer to the whole class. This method is geared toward the students helping each other. By assisting in teaching their fellow students, they are actually assisting in teaching themselves.

Instructors can also find that frequently stopping their presentations to engage their students in an activity can help them to process the information much faster. When a presentation builds using context learning as well, the results benefit from a combination of learning methods.

Accelerated learning focused on the end game of acquiring a new skill or additional knowledge. One does not need to use every learning method, just the best combination for the student to truly immerse themselves into the learning process.

As we have seen, accelerated learning is about using a variety of methods, recognizing that the students will often dictate what works the best for them. Still there are some guidelines that must be mentioned when discussing accelerated learning. We will cover these guiding principles in the next chapter.

Chapter 2: About N-L-P

Before we can delve deeper into the applications, advantages and methods of performing NLP techniques, we must first look at some basic parameters and outline a fundamental framework of the constituents constituting this technique making it easier to grasp the methodology.

Neurology:

Neurology refers to the working of the human nervous system. Before we focus on that, we need to first look at the components of the nervous system, mainly the central nervous system- dealing with the direct acts of thinking, storing and compartmentalizing information and planning and implementing actions- and the peripheral nervous system, which is responsible for the reflexive actions taken in sudden, unexpected situations, which do not require pre-processed thoughts.

Let us have a look now at how the CNS functions. The CNS is the root of all of a human's ideas, judgment and perception.

When in a situation, our central nervous system analyzes the situation it finds itself in, and based on either two of the following it executes certain actions, making our body respond in particular ways:

Based on previous experiences: Experiences which are stored in our brain can be called upon, to guide the mind in taking decisions in similar seeming situations.

Based on surrounding environment: In cases where there is no prior experience of an event, the human brain conjures up a solution which is deeply rooted in the bringing up which we have gone through, and the environment the human being has been subjected to.

As is evident, everything from experiences to environment gets stored in the human brain, and affects our way of thinking. Due to this, two humans going through similar situations may find themselves employing entirely different approaches on how to go about handling said situation. This variance arises mainly due to the difference in perception.

It thus becomes important to be able to compartmentalize and retrieve this information in an efficient, effective manner. NLP helps us in doing just that.

Language:

Linguistics is the second parameter in NLP. In primitive terms, linguistics is the study of language. Here, it refers to the medium adopted to convey our thoughts into actions and to express our views. Though it may sound over-hyped, language is probably the most important part of having an effective and realistic goal achieving.

One of the major drawbacks people face today is that of miscommunication. They are unable to express their views clearly, and even they attempt, they end up speaking before thinking. This oftentimes leads to a mixed reaction from the recipient of the message, and hence hinders the efficiency of the mind of the sender. While this pertains to external communication, the same importance must be given to internal communication, as there is a continuous and constant monologue ongoing in the background of the human mind, be it while decision making, or while comprehending a situation. For this reason, internal communication needs to be clear, comprehensive and precise.

Programming:

Once the mind and our linguistics have been optimized to achieve full results, they need to be coordinated together, in order to train the mind to work in the best possible way, which is done through programming, and having control command over our mind & language.

The first step is to organize our thoughts, feelings and ideas, in order to increase the efficiency of the brain. As the saying goes "A cluttered mind is the devil's workshop"! A clutter in the storage room of the body can lead to unwanted, undesirable emotional outburst at inconvenient times, thereby obstructing the efficiency of a person, in either professional or personal fields.

It is here where programming helps by keeping in control the emotions, disallowing them to interfere in a particular situation where it is not required. It so happens sometimes, that due to an overload of information the human brain can also sometimes get confused on how to produce the exact information required in a situation. In such a case, programming helps by compartmentalizing and categorizing stored information, so that information retrieval can be optimized.

The Three Levels of Mind:

Our mind consists of three parts: the conscious mind, the subconscious mind and the unconscious mind. The conscious mind is the current state of awareness, of the surroundings and the information pertaining to it. This data is readily accessible for use by the mind. The subconscious mind stores information which can be reached and retrieved with some level of difficulty. The information getting stored in the subconscious gets interpreted continuously by the brain, but the brain isn't actively aware of this.

This concept will be better explained through an example. When we find ourselves in a known environment, we automatically reach out without paying specific attention the environment, and conduct ourselves in a familiar manner. Similarly, when we speak in our native tongue, the words come automatically, without us having to put an extra effort to conjure those words.

Finally, the unconscious mind, which is responsible for our instincts, and those feelings we attribute to our gut instinct. This information, stored in the unconscious mind, isn't available as freely as the information stored in the conscious or the subconscious. Though it is unknown to us, it nevertheless affects our actions, as well as impulsive decision making.

NLP helps retrieve and access the data stored in the unconscious, by making a collection of facts based on past experiences, forming a data bank, and eventually making the information stored in the unconscious a part of the subconscious and finally the conscious mind.

Chapter 3: Have Self-Confidence

The idea of self-confidence usually utilized as confidence in one's close to home judgment, capacity, control, and so forth. One's self-confidence increments from encounters of having agreeably finished specific activities. It is a positive conviction that later on one can, for the most part, achieve what one wishes to do. Self-confidence isn't simply similar regard, which is one's very own assessment worth, while self-assurance is all the more explicitly trust in one's capacity to accomplish some objective, which one meta-examination proposed is like speculation of self-efficacy. Abraham Maslow and numerous others after him have underscored the need to recognize self-assurance as a summed up character trademark, and self-assurance as for a particular assignment, capacity or challenge (for example self-viability). Self-confidence regularly alludes to general self-assurance. This is not the same as self-viability, which therapist Albert Bandura has characterized as a "faith in one's capacity to prevail in explicit circumstances or achieve a task and along these lines is the term that all the more precisely alludes to explicit self-confidence. Analysts have since quite a while ago noticed that an individual can have self-confidence that the person in question can finish a particular errand (self-adequacy) (for example cook a decent dinner or compose a decent novel) despite the fact that they may need general selfassurance, or on the other hand act naturally certain however they come up short on the self-adequacy to accomplish a specific undertaking

2.1 Self-Compassion is important

Pardoning and supporting yourself can make way for better wellbeing, connections, and general prosperity. Self-compassion yields various advantages, including lower levels of uneasiness and discouragement. Self-compassion individuals perceive when they are enduring and are thought to themselves on these occasions, which decreases their uneasiness and related melancholy.

 While a few people drop without anyone else's input empathy normally, others need to learn it. Fortunately, it is learnable expertise.

Harvard analyst Christopher Germer, in his book The Mindful Path to SelfCompassion, recommends that there are five different ways to bring Selfcompassion into your life: by means of physical, mental, passionate, social, and profound strategies. He and different specialists have proposed an assortment of approaches to encourage Self-compassion. Here is a couple:

☐Solace your body. Eat something sound. Rests and rest your body. Back rub your own neck, feet, or hands. Go for a stroll. Anything you can do to improve how you feel physically gives you a portion of Self-compassion.

☐Compose a letter to yourself. Depict a circumstance that made you feel torment (a separation with a sweetheart, an occupation misfortune, an ineffectively gotten introduction). Compose a letter to yourself portraying the circumstance without accusing anybody. Recognize your sentiments.

□ Give yourself support. On the off chance that something awful or excruciating transpires, consider what you would state to a decent companion if something very similar transpired or her. Direct these humane reactions toward yourself.

□ Practice care. This is the nonjudgmental perception of your own considerations, emotions, and activities, without attempting to stifle or deny them. At the point when you look in the mirror and don't care for what you see, acknowledge the awful with the great with a merciful disposition.

2.2 So is Self-Doubt

Self-doubt can be a disturbing and convincing voice that keeps you down. It keeps you away from taking advantage of your lucky breaks. It makes the beginning or completing things harder than they should be.

Of course, it can some of the time be valuable as it encourages you to calmly observe your present constraints or just perceive an insane or poorly conceived notion. Be that as it may, for the most part, it keeps you down throughout everyday life.

So how might you get around that, how might you conquer those seasons of selfquestion with the goal that you can push ahead by and by?

1. State stop.

To start with, when your inward questions bubble up, be speedy. Try not to let them turn wild or develop from a murmur to a surge of debilitating sentences. Rather, the disrespect that far-fetched some portion of yourself.

In your psyche, state or yell something like No, no, no, we are not going down that street once more.

By doing so you can upset the idea example and prevent that internal identity skeptic from dominating.

2. Look to the past and flooded yourself in the recollections.

Be genuine with yourself and ask yourself: How often when I questioned myself or dreaded something would happen did that negative thing come into reality after regardless I made a move? The response for me – and most likely for you as well – isn't regularly by any stretch of the imagination.

Self-questions are frequently only beasts in your mind that your brain may use to prevent you from making changes and to keep you inside a safe place. On the off chance that you look to the past and perceive how well things have gone ordinarily in spite of those self-questions then it becomes simpler to relinquish them or to disregard them and to concentrate on the almost certain positive result and to make a move.

3. Converse with somebody about it.

At the point when you keep your considerations within they can get twisted, misrepresented and not particularly in accordance with the real world or sensible desires.

This is especially evident with regard to self-questioning considerations. So let them out into the light. Converse with somebody near you about your selfquestions.

Simply allowing them to out and saying them for all to hear can frequently assist you with hearing how misrepresented these considerations have become. What's more, by discussing those questions with somebody that is strong you can get an adjustment in context.

4. Try not to stall out in the correlation trap.

In the event that you contrast yourself with others very regularly, to their victories and particularly to the high-light reels that they share via web-based networking media then self-uncertainty can rapidly crawl up.

A superior approach to things is to contrast yourself with yourself. To perceive how far you have come. To perceive what you've survived. What's more, to perceive how you've continued onward, succeeded and

developed as a person.
5. Start keeping a diary.
Keeping a diary can be a useful propensity for some reasons. With regards to selfquestions, it can push you to:

Keep a sensible record of your life. Furthermore, help you to recollect the positive things, the triumphs you have had and how you have beaten hindrances on the off chance that you are inclined to recalling things with a negative inclination.

Increase lucidity all the more effectively. It is frequently simpler to mitigate fears and questions and to pick up clearness in the event that you have an issue spread out on paper or in a PC archive as opposed to on the off chance that you attempt to experience it all in your brain. By making arrangements of advantages and disadvantages, experiencing your musings and feelings and comparable occasions from an earlier time and by recording alternate points of view on the issue it gets simpler to discover arrangements and to see your test in a clearer and progressively prudent manner.

6. Keep in mind: individuals couldn't care less that much about what you do or say.

At the point when you stress over what others may think or state on the off chance that you accomplish something, at that point oneself uncertainty can immediately get more grounded and you stall out in inaction and in dread.

At the point when that happens advice yourself that truly individuals don't generally think that much about what you do or not do.

They have their hands full of pondering themselves, their children and pets, employments and up and coming games matches and stressing over what individuals may consider them.

7. What somebody said or did probably won't be about you (or about what you think it is).

At the point when somebody scrutinizes you at that point, it's anything but difficult to begin questioning yourself.

At the point when somebody rejects you and you don't get a second date after that initial one that you think went entirely well at that point it's not all that abnormal to get down on yourself.

Be that as it may, imagine a scenario where what the person in question said or did isn't generally about you by any means.

Maybe your colleague that verbally lashed out at you is having an awful day, month or marriage.

Furthermore, you probably won't have gotten that second date in light of the fact that the other individual's mother became ill and he needed to concentrate on that or in light of the fact that he reconnected with his ex and needed to give their relationship another shot.

You don't know it all that is going on in someone else's life. What's more, the world doesn't spin around you. So be cautious so you don't misjudge and assemble fault and uncertainty inside with no explanation.

8. Get an increase in confidence.
Let another person's excitement, inspiration, and helpful good faith stream over to you.

Go through 20 minutes with a book recording, a webcast or a book that gives you that. Tim Ferriss' digital broadcast has helped me with this as of late and I've throughout the years regularly tuned in to book recordings by Brian Tracy to get this lift.

This fast brief session can extraordinarily assist you with shifting your selfquestions into good faith and into considering your test.

9. Consider a to be as impermanent.

At the point when you have a mishap then you may begin to see things through a negative and dull focal point. You may consider this to be a misfortune as something that will just be your new ordinary.

Along these lines of seeing things can trap you in believing that there's no reason for proceeding to make a move.

So all things being equal:

Keep in mind: You are not a disappointment since you fizzled. Misfortunes happen to everybody who takes risks. It is just a piece of living completely. Some of the time things work out in a good way and in some cases, they don't. So don't make a disappointment into this gigantic thing or into your character.

Ask yourself: what is one thing I can gain from this difficulty? Utilize the slip-up or inability furthering your potential benefit and to push ahead indeed in a more astute manner.

10.   Hone   your   abilities.
 In the event that you, for example, frequently get self-question before an introduction in school or at work at that point hone your introduction abilities.

Peruse a couple of books about it and practice at home before a mirror or before a companion. Or on the other hand, join Toastmasters to get the experience or information you need.

 At that point, you'll feel increasingly certain, equipped and loose in such circumstances.

 11. Try not to whip yourself about it.

A typical method to deal with self-question is to blow up at yourself and your absence of movement. To attempt to pound yourself as an approach to get yourself to push ahead.

That doesn't – as far as I can tell – help that much.

I have discovered that being benevolent and productive when feeling selfquestion is a superior decision. So I utilize kind and understanding words towards myself however I likewise ask myself:

What is one little advance I can take to push ahead in this circumstance? At that point, I make that extremely little stride and begin to bit by bit move towards where I need to go.

12. Praise that little advance and win.

At the point when you've stepped forward – for instance, set up your very own site or gone for the first brief run in quite a while or years – and you're finished with it then you have a success. It might be a little one yet it's as yet a success. So commend it.

Have a scrumptious tidbit or your preferred nourishment for supper, invest some energy in your preferred leisure activity or get yourself something you've needed for quite a while.

This will reestablish and revive your inspiration and make making a movie feel all the more energizing and fun. Furthermore, that will propel self-questions aside with the goal that you can continue moving and get all the more little and greater successes.

13. Remember: You can course-correct along the way.
Attempting to design each move you will make on a voyage towards an objective or dream can get depleting and lead to a considerable amount of self-question.

Also, it, for the most part, don't work that well in any case since the best-laid plans frequently begin to self-destruct a piece or need some change when they are gone up against the real world.

So do a touch of harsh arranging and afterward start your voyage.

What's more, recall that you can generally course-address en route towards what you need. Engaged by the new information, experience and input you will get as you prop up on that way.

2.3 Perform Behavioral Experiments

Behavioral experiments provide a way to deal with testing unhelpful convictions about rest and creating/testing new (and supportive) convictions about rest, and a way to deal with encouraging consciousness of sustaining subjective and social procedures and realizing a change in/inversion of these procedures. In light of clinical experience, this treatment methodology might be hard to use when the setting takes into consideration short treatment sessions in light of the fact that most behavioral experiments need time to set up and afterward, in an ensuing session, question. Since verbal strategies like straightforwardly scrutinizing the coherent premise of considerations and convictions, Socratic addressing, and guided disclosure are regularly insufficient all alone to achieve significant change, social analyses are utilized. Behavioral experiments are arranged experiential exercises, in light of experimentation or perception, which are attempted by patients in or between treatment sessions. Their plan is gotten straightforwardly from detailing the issue, and their main role is to get new data, which adds to the improvement and check of the definition.

Chapter 4: Challenging Your Lifestyle

Goals

In the previous chapter, I asked you to look at yourself, both internally and externally. To progress in life, you need to care for your body, mind, and soul. Only then can you achieve your life goals. If your diet consists of too much junk food, you most likely already know that type of diet is not good for you. It's time to take a close look at your present lifestyle and make some improvements. Ask yourself questions such as:

·Do you sleep well?

·How do you cope with stress?

·What is your exercise regime?

·How organized is your week's agenda?

Be honest in your answers because if you're not, you are only letting yourself down. You MUST tackle your own shortcomings before you can begin your new lifestyle. A healthy body is a healthy mind. Most importantly, for the topic of this book, a healthy mind means you can begin to speed-learn and become successful at it.

To help you get started, here are a few basic lifestyle habits you need to look at:

Time Management

Any improvements in your lifestyle goals will be based on the solid foundation of organized time management. Dissect a week in your typical routine of life, only then can you see where the shortfalls are. For the first week, write down everything you do every hour. Make a chart that covers all seven days and all 24-hours. What is it that you're looking for?

At the end of the week when you assess your chart, you will be identifying:

·Gaps where you can introduce short bursts of physical exercise. Even if it means only a short brisk walk, this is better than sitting at a desk or doing nothing.

·Write down everything that you eat because it is very true that you are what you eat and drink. Your digestive system is breaking your food down into the good, bad and downright ugly. It's now time to make sure that there is more "goodness" entering your body.

·Record the times you go to bed and what time you get up. Make a note of any times that you feel a need to get up during the night. Also, jot down what you do when you get up. Do you have a habit of nighttime snacks? Are you visiting the toilet? Are you having trouble sleeping? These are all the situations you are looking to identify.

·Jot down a few words about the moods you are feeling. You don't need to write detailed emotions, but you are looking to see what effects your mood swings. You could simply use a code, such as:

H for Happy

D for Depressed

F for fed up

Add a few of your own for the in-between emotions.

This will help you recognize if stress or depression is a problem in your life.

The idea of this whole concept is to find all your weaknesses and bad habits. Once you know them, you can tackle them and change your whole life around.

What does this have to do with fast-track learning?

Everything!

You are beginning your self-discipline routine by going right back to the basics.

Dietary Assessment

There are so many different cultural recipes and ways of eating that I cannot cover all the various diets everywhere in the world. What is generally agreed upon is that we need to ingest healthy natural foods. To compliment this guideline, we need to eat less unhealthy processed foods.

Food is like a fashion and goes through many fads. To enjoy a healthy diet, you need to ignore the fads and follow your own knowledge and common sense. Most of us know the sensible options, but choose to ignore the obvious. Don't eat too much junk food. This covers take-outs, fast food, processed foods, and sugary foods.

Not only will such foods increase your weight, but they will fog your brain instead of enhancing it. This is not a book about dietary needs, but high carb foods will cause your body to produce the wrong hormones. With stored up fats, you will gain weight, leading to that terrible feeling of lethargy. This is the road to ill health. Make some ground rules for yourself with regards to your dietary intake, such as:

·Stick to three meals a day and try NOT to snack between. Breakfast can be a quick healthy smoothie. Lunch should be made at home and not shop bought. Make sure your last meal has digested long before you go to bed.

·If you don't know how to home cook, then learn. Using your own ingredients is far healthier than shop bought meals. They can be full of hidden sugars and salt. Take lunch to work with you, so a take-out does not tempt you. You'll also save money by making your own meals.

·You must eat plenty of vegetables. Call them your brain food, and the darker they are, the more vitamins they contain. Eat fruit too, such as lots of berries that don't contain high concentrates of natural glucose sugars.

·Cut down on your meat intake, not only for your own health but for the environment too. Most specifically red meat. Meat has lots of protein, which is great brain food, but you can also get protein in many other healthy foods.

·Contrary to recent fads, not all fat is bad for you. It's making sure you are eating the right type of fats. You do not need to avoid foods with fats, just learn your good fats from your bad ones. Cook with olive oil. Avoid excess animal fats, including too much dairy products. Don't drink sugary drinks such as sodas and hot chocolate.

·As with sugar and carbohydrates, keep your alcohol and caffeine intake low.

These are but a few tips on healthy eating. Do your research and understand the food you are putting into your body. It is believed that a Mediterranean diet can feed the brain and keep you healthy.

Exercise

Latest figures claim that only 28% of Americans meet the recommended National Physical Activity Guide. With such reports, the chances are that you are guilty of not exercising your body enough.

You don't need to dash out and join an expensive gym. With a little imagination, it can cost nothing to keep your body fit. Your new regime should include the minimum recommendation. That is 150-minutes of moderate exercise, plus 75-minutes of vigorous exercise. It only amounts to under 4-hours per week. This is achievable for most people.

This is where the diary of your weekly agenda will be useful. Please note, this is not about losing weight because exercise alone will not achieve that. This is about the least amount of exercise you should be doing for your heart, muscles, and joints. Anything less is a health risk to your body. If you could incorporate at least 5 x 30-minute walks into your week, you've already covered the 150-minutes. The 75-minute needs to get your heart pumping. Add another 2 x 35-minute very brisk walks to your weekly schedule, and you've done it. That's how easy it can be. Of course, it would be better if you could do more. It would also be better if you made the 75-minutes into something a little more vigorous for your muscles. Something that will tax your body a little more.

Sleep

By making these great improvements to your health, you should find that you sleep better too. Quality sleep is as important as good food and exercise. If you see that you're not getting the recommended 6-8-hours sleep, then you need to investigate what's bothering you. Stress-related worries can keep us all awake at night. If this sounds familiar to you, then you must not let these problems linger on for too long. Your new lifestyle covers many areas of your health. Consider your sleeping pattern as your personal battery charger. If it's not working properly, it needs fixing.

State of Mind

This follows on from the topic of Sleeping quite well because if you're not relaxed at the end of your day, your state of mind will not be in a healthy place. Most of us have stress in our lives, and it's not something that is easy to avoid. Instead, you need to learn how to do deal with it. If you ignore it, you are taking a risk with your health and may become ill. Your mental health is just as important as your physical health, so be proactive and take care of your mind. Learn some relaxation techniques for those moments when you get to wind down after a busy day. I know I said the brain is an amazing organ, but you still need to take care of it. Dealing with problems is much healthier than ignoring them. Do yourself a favor and look to resolve any of life's problems head-on. Your mind can function to its fullest potential as long as you're not bogged down with negative thoughts.

Relaxation Exercises

Some refer to these exercises as meditation because it means you can reflect upon your inner thoughts. It is a positive move to concentrate on your inner wellbeing. Such exercises can get you closer to understanding yourself.

Learn simple breathing techniques that you can do anywhere, anytime, such as the "4-7-8."

·Close your eyes and mouth.

·Take a deep breath through your nose, while you count to 4.

·Allow the intake of air to push out your stomach and lift your chest.

·Hold the breath and count to 7.

·Exhale the air out of an open mouth, while you count to 8.

·As you are repeating this exercise for a few minutes, clear your mind of what's going on around you. Visualize a sandy shore of the warm sun on your face.

·Repeat until your mind feels clear.

This is an exercise you can perform whenever you need a quick break from a busy schedule. Do it on a bus, in a tube, sat at your desk, in the toilet. It can be a lifesaver if you are feeling stressed. When you come out of the exercise, you should feel ready to face the world for a short while.

Added to this, you could also learn how to relax muscles throughout your body. It's good if you can lay down and work your way through your body from head to toe. If not, then focus on only a few muscles at a time.

•Start by concentrating on your feet and wiggle your toes. Clench any muscles you can feel in the foot and squeeze for around 5 seconds before you relax. Move your ankles around in circles.

•Make your way up your body. Next, do the squeezing in your calf muscles. Going on to the thigh, bottom, stomach chest, biceps, lower arm, fingers, hands and wrist, shoulders and neck. Finish off with the facial area.

•Pull distorted faces to get those facial muscles tense. Once you squeezed them for around 5 seconds, and then relax. You'll be amazed how refreshed your body feels after you've completed this exercise. If you don't have the time to lay down, try doing it on and off throughout your day when you're sitting down. Work your way through your body muscles, but concentrating on only one part of the body whenever you have a moment to spare.

These are some simple techniques to set about improving your present lifestyle. Get yourself into peak condition. Once you have a healthy regime, it's time to begin your speed learning practices.

Chapter 5: It's Not You It's Me:

Destructive Study Habits that are

Hindering Your Learning

The biggest problem with doing things the way they have always been done is that – you are doing them the way they have always been done. Remember in the last chapter when I pointed out that the definition of insanity is to do the same thing and expect a different result? It also applies here.

Perhaps you have a learning or studying routine that you carefully stick with. Perhaps it's the same routine that your father did when he was in school. Perhaps it's the routine that your best friend recommends, or your teacher or professor swear by. Either way, you know it's not working for you as you want it to, but you are repeating the process simply because that is what you have always done, so why change?

Without even realizing it, many adults and students alike engage in very destructive habits. In essence, they are holding themselves back from what they could be achieving, though they are doing their best to keep moving forward.

What are destructive study habits? Let's take a look at some of the most common culprits now:

Studying is viewed as a chore or a task – something to be done and over with rather than something to be enjoyed.

Study hall is often selected as a place to study – when it may not be ideal – if you are going to study, you have to be in the right environment. This means you need quiet, low activity, and no distractions.

Studying is both over and under prepared for – stop bringing your handheld gaming device and forgetting your calculator. Set yourself up for success rather than failure.

Techniques learned in earlier schooling are ignored – there was a reason you were taught how to make diagrams, outlines, and write drafts. They may not by the most fun thing to do, but neglecting to formulate your material and your thoughts results in poor memory of the material you are studying.

Studying is treated as a "fix–it–and–forget–it" subject – in other words, your brain can't lift the weight of the material if you haven't strengthened it with other exercises. Just as your body needs to grow accustomed to heavier weight before you can lift more, your mind needs to be exercised to better retain the information you pile into it.

Study is done with friends – or without them (whichever is worse) – there are those who simply must have someone there to help them stay focused on the topic at hand while they are studying, then there are those who desperately need to be alone so they can concentrate.

Even though this is common, it is also common to find that people who need one method of studying are often implementing the others – those who should be with friends are alone, and those who really should be studying alone are doing it with friends (and thus ending up distracted.)

While accelerated learning is something that is personal, and the results are going to be subjective to the individual who is engaging in the form of study, there are key principles that need to be identified and addressed in everyone's lives.

For example:

There is a classroom full of students, each one with the directive to study for the upcoming exam.

One student immediately puts in his earphones and listens to music as he flips through his book. Another student pulls out a pen and blank paper and doodles on the paper as she reads through the material.

There are students who are quietly reading the material out loud to themselves, and there are students who are glancing around the book, but look bored.

Each student has resorted to using the best study method they know how – there is no universal answer. However, if you were to walk into the room and change up the study techniques– say, give the person who needs quiet the earphones and give the student who is easily distracted the pencil and paper, you are going to quickly have a mess on your hands.

It's not that some of the study methods are better than others, it's that each person has their own unique style with their study, and, each person has their own unique needs for their study. Accelerated learning is designed to help each person who uses it identify what it is they need in their own lives, and help them address that with new techniques that work.

Some say it's complicated, others argue that it is no more effective than any other form of learning, but the results speak for themselves. As you know, your method of learning right now isn't working for you, and you do need someone to help point you in the right direction and give you the boost that you need. Accelerated learning is going to do that very thing, and I am going to show you how.

Chapter 6: Optimal Cognitive Function

To keep the body in good health is a duty ...
other wise we shall not be able to keep our mind strong and clear. "

-Buddha
 Healthy Brain Lifestyle

This chapter reminds us just how important it is to have a healthy functioning brain and understanding how it affects memory and our cognitive functions. There are many variables in your life that can affect your brain and your overall health.

Here are the most common factors to having the health you were intended to have. To fulfill your purpose and to have an optimal memory experience you must pay attention to the simple variables that you must gain control over for massive results.

Balanced Nutrition

Your brain needs fuel in order to function. No tissue in the body can ever function properly without adequate nutrition – and the brain is no exception. In fact, among all the organs in the body, the brain is one of what works the most. As such, it needs a lot of nutrients. Feed it by eating a well-balanced diet that satisfies the energy and nutrient requirements of all tissues, including the brain.

To achieve a balanced diet, you must eat a variety of foods from each of the food groups. Our bodies react to what we put in it; good and bad. Find out what nutrition you're having a lack of; you need to supplement what ever your body isn't getting.

Your brain is 73% water. Water alone is the most basic essential and it takes only 2% dehydration to affect your attention, memory, and other cognitive skills.

Loss of fatty acids DHA and EPA are found linked to depression, Parkinson, and Alzheimers. Imagine what else can profoundly affect how you feel and function.

Gut   Health
and   the   Brain   Connection
There is an inextricable connection between the gut and the brain. One surprising fact is that the gut and the brain develop from the same embryonic tissue during the fetal stage.

Another proof of the brain and gut connection is the presence of the ENS or enteric nervous system. The ENS functions similarly to the brain, but for a totally different purpose. This "little brain" residing in the gut is composed of 2 thin layers with over 100 million nerve cells. This ENS lines the entire length of the gut, starting from the esophagus down to the rectum.

What it does is control everything involved in the digestive process. It controls the release of the digestive enzymes, coordinates swallowing and the entire peristaltic movement of the gut controls the flow of blood to and from the gut and ensures elimination and nutrient absorption. This system controls how much nutrients are released from the food through digestion and how much nutrients enter the blood for distribution.

If the ENS is not functioning well, there won't be enough nutrients to reach the tissues, including the brain.

One factor that can contribute to this is inflammation of the gut, which can lead to the so-called brain fog. This, in turn, will affect memory and cause you to become less attentive, focus poorly, and forget things more often. It's your role to find out what your body needs and if this could be something effecting you; and by then you would take supplements or vitamins that promote gut health and Inflammation like **Colostrum** or **L-Glutemine.**

All of these were discovered by a study made in Johns Hopkins Center for Neurogastroenterology. This study was able to establish a direct link between the gut and brain function. It was determined that the state and function of the gut affects how the brain carries out its several functions and vice versa. There is a deep connection between the two. They are constantly communicating and affecting each other in their functions.

Mental Stimulation

Challenges can be as simple as trying to use your non-dominant hand. If you are a right-handed person, you should occasionally use the left hand, and vice-versa. Try brushing your teeth, comb your hair, or dial your phone with your non-dominant hand every day. The goal is to challenge the brain by putting use to use every part of it. In the case of a right-handed person, he would be using his left brain most of the time, leaving too little stimulation for the right side.

This is the secret to feeling young and active at least, mentally. Mental stimulation keeps your brain sharp with great abilities to concentrate. This involves giving your brain a good challenge. The challenge can stimulate your brain, triggering more brain cells to function and creating more connections between the nerve cells and strengthening the existing connections.

Mental exercises should be stimulating – not excruciating. Another way to give your brain some stimulation is to try new things, like a new skill or a new hobby. You can try learning a programming language if you're already an expert computer user. You can even just travel and soak in the novel sights, sounds, and experiences.

Social interaction is another way to boost mental stimulation. We are social beings and need to particularly interact and should show interest in others, a little interaction can help balance your energy.

The ideal is to stimulate and challenge weak parts of the brain so we can experience whole brain power. There is a sense of a brighter awareness and clarity when we travel, learn, grow or become inspired. We need to push ourselves to experience this type of stimulation more often and read daily to remind us our unlimited abilities.

Physical Exercise

A study done at the University of British Columbia, the results of which are published in the British Journal of Sports medicine, cardiovascular exercises have been observed to have a positive effect on the size and performance of the hippocampus, which is that part of the brain that is used in learning and verbal memory. That is just one of the many studies that show that physical exercises like walking and running can also benefit the brain. These can improve cognitive functions and memory abilities. The improvements are brought about by the effects of physical exercise such as stimulation of growth factors, reduction of inflammation, and a decrease in insulin resistance. Exercise also fine-tunes several pathways, which enhances the release of brain chemicals that promote better brain health, new growth of blood vessels, and growth and survival of brain cells.

Sleep   vs   Resting

To have a proper rejuvenating night of sleep, you need to exhort a certain amount of energy during the day so you can fall asleep with ease. 7-9 hours of sleep is recommended but you can have 9 hours restless sleep and still continue to feel groggy all day. It is also possible to have 5 hours of deep, restful sleep and wake up with enough energy to tackle the day from better quality rest.

Make your room a sleep sanctuary. Turn off all the electronics; sleeping with the TV on has a big effect on your sleep and dreams. It's recommended to put the phone far from your bed. Make your room dark as possible. Stop hitting the snooze button; get use to getting up out of your bed at the first sign of waking from an alarm.

To promote good sleep quality, your room should be a sleep sanctuary. It should be used solely for sleeping, not for other activities like work. In fact, never take work or work materials with you to your bed.

Also, all gadgets should also be turned off. Studies showed that exposure to blue light, such as from electronic devices, prevent the brain from resting and getting restful sleep. The electric fields emitted by these devices interfere with the body's own bio-communication process. This interruption prevents you from getting a truly restful sleep.

Other tips to promote restful sleep include darkening the room and removing any stimuli like the television and radio. You can also promote better oxygenation in the room by adding more indoor plants or using a humidifier. Keep the room temperature comfortable by using either cooling appliances like air conditioners and fans or warming devices like indoor heaters.

Consolidates Memories Overnight

The brain clears out toxins; it also creates and consolidates memories. Be aware of what you listen to or watch before going to bed it can have a negative or positive affect on your sleep.

If you're looking to boost your memory to do better in school, remember that studying before bed has been proven to help recall what was studied for the big exam.

Also, note that an unconscious resting state can make surprising new connections which mean more ah-ha moments. Practice something challenging before bed, the next morning you should feel like you have made big improvement effortlessly.

Reducing   Stress

It is vital in your everyday life to reduce stress for maintaining your overall health, as it can improve your overall mood, perspective, immune system and productivity.

When you become stressed, your brain experiences both chemical and physical changes that affect its overall functioning. Pay close attention during periods of high stress, certain chemicals within the brain, including the neurotransmitters dopamine, epinephrine, cortisol, and norepinephrine begin to rise, causing larger amounts of these and other "fight-or-flight" hormones such as adrenalin to be released by the adrenal glands. Combating Stress & Performing Better We're all familiar with tension and the inability to think clearly that occurs during stressful situations. However, did you know that they may be symptoms of imbalanced cortisol levels that result from too much stress and anxiety? Adrenal fatigue syndrome occurs when adrenal glands don't function properly, usually due to prolonged environmental, physical, or emotional stress. It's no surprise that those situations trigger the release of the "stress hormone," cortisol. Elevated cortisol levels can even result from heavy exertion during strenuous exercise or from just having a lot on your plate in life. The release of these chemicals contributes to certain physiological effects, including rapid heart rate, higher blood pressure, and a weakened immune system.

So, what can you do to shift yourself into a healthier pattern and reduce stress? One of the most effective and rewarding techniques is meditation. encourage yourself to relax your mind and examine your inner self to notice signs of stress or anxiety.

Breathing exercises can be very beneficial to change your state immediately.

Also, try to spend less time around people that can make you feel stress, angry or uncomfortable, people that gossip or always complain and talk bad about other can make you feel stressed without even noticing. You may even pick up the habit to gossip as well, it's important to surround yourself daily in environments that you can experience a sense of flow. It's recommended to create a morning/daily routine that helps manage your stress levels and puts you in a focused state of mind to handle your daily demands.

The Power of Supplementing Ramp Up Attention, Memory, Learning, & Cognition

Whether you're experiencing cognitive decline or simply looking to get more from your mind, there are supplements you should be taking based on what you think you need. For example; **phosphatidylserine** can help Improve the ease of electrical impulses flowing between cells, this compound strengthens the inner cell membrane and directly enhances communication between brain cells. This effect not only reduces brain fog, but it also improves clarity of thought, memory, rates of learning, alertness, attention, and overall cognition. Phosphatidylserine protects you from stress by reducing cortisol levels during taxing times. The importance of supplementing cannot be emphasized enough.

Nootropic Supplements

A nootropic is a supplement that enhances cognitive function. A nootropic can act to increase memory, concentration, motivation, mood. The brain needs nutrition/brain food to function at its best capability, the nootropic just supplements what ever is missing your diet. Some nootropics are a stack of great nutrients for the brain, so if you have been experiencing a lack of focus or concentration, then you should look into nootropics your self. Alpha Brain and Focus factor are some of the most popular, do your own research to learn more.

Memory And The Lucid Dreamer
Nootropics and nutritional dieting can help you have clearer dreams and increase your chances of having lucid dreams. Practice prospective memory in your daily life.

prospective memory : The forward-thinking ability to **remember to remember.**

You already do this on a daily basis; you only have to be more aware of your actions now. Examples of these prospective memory tasks include remembering you have something important to follow through on or pay bills. You need to practice this with more awareness.

With the memory reality check -you try to remember what just happened in the past few minutes, and what happened a few moments ago. These reality checks are happening though out the day and you can do any type of check, the point is to do the same check in your dreams to realize its only a dream. Most often we don't realize when we are in a dream because we don't practice reality checks. Prospective memory will help with reality checks and help recall dreams after you have awakened by which giving you more chances to have lucid dreams.

Chapter 7: Some of the Slowdowns of

Reading

There are many things besides poor training as a child that can be contributing to your lack of speed when it comes to reading and comprehension. Knowing the roadblocks that are sitting in front of you is the best way to learn how to get around them with ease and aplomb. There are many small things that can be getting in the way of your long term goals without you even realizing it. Here are a few of them to keep in mind as you are learning to read faster and expand your horizons.

Learn to Pay Attention

The first problem that is most likely holding you up from the success that you are looking for is simply just learning to pay attention. It's so easy to get distracted from what you are doing, especially if the material is at all dry. Learning to focus properly and remove distractions from your immediate area will go a long way in improving your rate of reading and your comprehension.

Talking to Yourself

Many people get caught up in bad habits at a very young age and one of these habits that can be slowing you down might be reading out loud. You may be either vocalizing out loud or sub-vocalizing, however, either one will slow you down because it means that you can only read as fast as you can speak. When you read with only your eyes and brain, you can really get that speed up there.

Stopping Too Often

When you are reading material, studies have shown that your eye make loops along the line of text in order to tie the whole thought together. People who read at a slower speed or those that have problems with comprehension do this on a much higher scale than others. The more often you experience these stops in your overall reading, the slower your actual pace will be.

Re-reading the Same Phrase

It can slow you down when you have to read the same information over and over. If you read it once, then it is generally shown to be more effective than trying to go back and grasp things that you think you missed. If you get through the whole passage and then still feel like you don't understand it, then you can go back to it, but try to limit yourself to one read through at first.

Change Up Your Speed

If you have trouble with reading then you generally read at the same pace no matter what. However, more efficient readers slow down their pace through the difficult pieces and speed it back up again once they get to the easier portions. A lot of passages have filler words to make them grammatically correct or unimportant text to make the writing more colloquial. If you can get through those parts at a faster speed then you can gather the information needed at a faster rate.

Remember, these are just a few common problems that people run into when they are trying to read an assortment of things.

You may have your own unique issues as well, but at least use this information as a starting point in order to pinpoint what is slowing you down. Next, we will move on to steps to actually speed up your reading rate, however, it's important that you address the behaviors that can stop your progress.

Chapter 8: MAIN IDEAS OF ACCELERATED

LEARNING

Learning includes mind and body in their entirety Holistic, multidimensional teaching design

Learning is creating, not consuming

Collaboration promotes learning Participant Centering / Interpersonal Learning / Social Learning in Groups

Learning happens on many levels at the same time

Learning springs from doing the actual work (with feedback) Learning springs from doing the real work (with feedback)

Positive emotions promote learning twice

The figurative brain captures information instantly and automatically Demonstrate and visualize

Learning springs from doing the actual work (with feedback) Participation/partnership, cooperative teaching

What are the main thoughts of Accelerated Learning?

1. Pay attention not only to a large amount of substance, but to the anchoring of the substance

Most coaches try to convey as much material as possible to the participants in the time available. They often achieve the opposite, that is, hardly anything gets stuck and the whole training is not effective. It makes more sense to pay more attention to a good anchoring of the content in the long-term memory, which can be achieved through exercises and repetitions. After information phases, plan repetitive exercises and repetitive exercises. Think of many creative ways to repeat content.

2. Learning can and should be fun

Try to create a positive learning environment. Include interesting tasks and games in the training. Use group work for content development. Make each training sequence varied and exciting. Create curiosity among the participants. You can also use music in the seminar. If the participants switch off, they are doing something wrong.

3. Try to work up the contents according to the brain

Create a stress-free and positive learning environment. Try to address all types of learning (learning by listening, seeing, doing). Make active activities and physical exercises part of your workout. Use the learning in small groups or teams again and again. Use many demo materials, visualizations and music in the seminar. Offer the participants tips.

4. Switch between active and passive learning activities

Long passivity leads to fatigue of the body and mind of the participants. If you are tired, you will not be able to absorb any more content and the training will become unproductive. Try to implement active learning units (exercises, repetitions, group work) over and over again.

5. Create a positive learning community

A positive group atmosphere among the participants promotes learning. Try to do group work again and again. Take influence on the group atmosphere.

6. Use peripheral information

Peripheral information is wall decorations, posts, pictograms, etc. These visualizations have the advantage that they are always visible in the room and thus better anchored in the memory.

7. Involve the participants actively in learning

Learning is not pure consumption, but the participants themselves have to embed new knowledge in existing structures and to think about their implementation. Also, the participants should be able to influence the learning process. Ask the expectations of the participants and regularly reflect on the learning process with the participants.

Chapter 9: Understanding Yourself as a

Learner

Many of us understand the genre of books we enjoy reading. A few people enjoy thrillers and do not like science fiction; another group would rather read biographies or historical books. This is also applicable to our eating habits. You may like Indian or Chinese food, vegetarian or nonvegetarian, rice and potatoes, the list goes on.

What about learning then? To be an efficient learner, you are required to be familiar with the kind of learner you are. If you don't make out time to discover more, you may just be deluding yourself with the thoughts that you are incapable of doing something when you actually can. What makes you and your learning style unique? And what can you do to improve these areas in you that are underdeveloped?

These are the three key determinants of your style of learning:

1. Where you choose to learn

2. How easy it is for you to assimilate information

3. How you handle the information already assimilated

We have discussed the first determinant earlier. You now need to reflect on the impact the other two determinants have on your life.

We all thrive under separate environments, assimilate information differently, and handle it in our own unique ways. Neither John nor John is better than the other; both possess relevant skills for both the workplace and the home.

We would discuss how information enters the brain initially

How Information Is Assimilated

Your five senses are important in helping you assimilate information. Four of these senses are assimilated through the primitive brain, the brainstem; they are hearing, taste, touch, and some of the sight.

Smell, however, goes directly into the amygdala and the olfactory nerves in the limbic system, or the mammalian brain. Thus, the sense of smell is the fastest to be registered. Maybe our survival as a species is based on our ability to differentiate meat that smells "wrong" or the scent of our competitors!

Usually, one sense predominates over the others

Utilizing Your Senses

Commonly, the three ways of getting information are via your eyes, your ears or even through your body. You look at things, listen to things and get involved personally by experiencing them, most times involving touch. What is the best way for you to assimilate information? Using your eyes, your ears, or your body?

•Most times, do you have to sit up straight in meetings and try to look directly in the speaker's eye?

•Would you rather read than being read to, often grabbing information from others?

•Do you find it easy to remember a face always?

•Would you use maps or follow verbal instructions?

•Are your outfits usually coordinated?

•Are you quick to move to the charts and represent problems with drawings?

If your answer to a majority of these questions is yes, then you depend on your eyes most.

•Do you repeat words already spoken by a presenter or nod your head in affirmation when you are being spoken to?

•Do you sometimes stare into space and daydream while you carry on conversations in your mind?

•Do you enjoy listening to the radio and music?

•Do you ever forget a name?

•Would you rather follow verbal instructions?

•Do you tell jokes and fancy an engaging argument while solving a problem?

•Do you like using your phone?

If your answers to most of these questions is yes, then you are very dependent on your ears.

•Do you sometimes slouch on your chair during meetings upset that you are unable to wand up and move about?

•Do you enjoy fiddling with your pen, diary, paper, or with rubber when you are having a conversation?

•Do you enjoy outdoor adventures?

•Is it easier for you to remember events instead of people's names or faces?

•Do you make expressions with your body?

•Would you rather take action and fix things yourself instead of waiting around and talking about it?

•Do you like doing business and undertaking an activity concurrently?

Have you answered yes to the majority of these questions? If true, you are dependent mostly on your body.

A lot of people find it easier to assimilate information through these different ways. A few people, particularly those who have intentionally put in an effort to develop varying styles might prefer two or three of them. Ordinarily, in a group, about 30 percent of people will naturally be comfortable using their eyes; another 30 percent, their ears; and another thirty percent, their bodies. No single way is more efficient than the rest; they are all unique.

In many workplaces, dissemination of information is via writing or verbal instructions. In most training rooms, likewise meetings, people are not usually motivated to stand up and move around when this is exactly what a significant number of people would prefer to do.

Handling Information

The manner with which we handle the information absorbed by our senses depends on our personality. The person we are is a major factor in determining the way we discern information. To simplify it, two individuals can look at the same picture and see different things.

This is made even more evident when words are involved. When someone says to you, "That is a nice suggestion," you may hear one of these two options below:

That is a nice suggestion. Perfect! My conclusion, I am happy he agrees with me. I will proceed to book the plane tickets.

That's a nice suggestion. So is every other one we are looking at. We have to discover more to make a decision to either fly or take the train, or even rent a car and drive the entire team.

Carl Jung was the first to give a detailed explanation of this concept[2]. He categorized people into thinkers, sensors, feelers, and intuitors. Jung's ideas have formed the basis for most of the tests used to describe individual personality types. One of the most widely used is the Myer-Briggs personality test. Its objective is to discover an individual's natural preferences.

Sixteen basic personality types exist, based on four major types: intuitive thinkers, intuitive feelers, sensing thinkers, and sensing feelers. These four styles react in predictable and diverse ways when they collect information and act in reality. For instance, sensory thinkers would rather depend on irrefutable facts, whereas intuitors would prefer to depend on general impressions. One of the advantages of the Myer-Briggs personality test is that it is unbiased and is suitable for home as well as the workplace.

Figuring Out Your Learning Style

Peter Honey and Alan Mumford, both British psychologists, have invented a test [3]that is widely employed across various organizations. The test is based mainly on the three elements that contribute to a person's learning style, how information is processed. It proposes four learning styles: reflector, theorist, activist, and pragmatist

Without any further knowledge, which of them describes your learning personality best?

Honey and Mumford's explanations provide an approachable way you put the information you have assimilated into use. Though they do not explain the major component of a leading style, they provide an approachable and realistic point about your learning personality.

As an activist, you are the type of person that is quick to take charge and start. You like instantaneous experiences, and you are excited about new things. Most times you act first and think later. You enjoy engaging in activities, and as soon as you are presented with a problem, you begin devising different methods of solving it. You are probably a sociable person.

Your catchword is, "I'll attempt anything once."

As a reflector, you tend to avoid experiences. You would probably prefer to stay at the back in meetings. Before making any decision, you like to assimilate a variety of information. You like to stand back and see the direction of things before giving your ideas. You are very careful in nature

Your catchword is, "I'll have to think about that."

As a theorist, you tend to view things in a sequence, logically until you can make it into a pattern. You like systems, rules, and models. You like being unemotional and systematically. You are a deep thinker and will refuse to agree with an opinion just because it does not align with your point of view.

Your catchword is, "But how does it fit in with."

As a pragmatist, you are always eager to try out suggestions. You are very experimental. You would want to complete things quickly without wasting time. Once you hear something interesting, you want to experience it immediately

Your catchword is, "There must be a better way."

Chapter 10: Visual Techniques, Accelerate

Your Learning

Visual techniques are some of the most common learning techniques used in advanced learning. In the visual style of learning, a person is actually thinking in terms of pictures and images. It's almost as if he or she has installed a movie camera within the mind that captures all the information. When the learner wants to recall something, he simply dips into the reels of images he has stored in his mind.

Question: Is visual learning really helpful?

You bet. In the visual learning technique, everything is taken in the form of images and symbols. In a majority of people, breaking up information into images speeds up the process of learning by at least 60%. That means you can learn 60% faster than you previously did if you used visual techniques. According to research, a small percentage of children are instinctive visual learners. Such children are seen to do exceptionally well and can reproduce a lot of information with great ease.

The most commonly used visual techniques include:

Mind mapping

Semiotics

Linking

Chunking

Each of these techniques basically makes use of the mind's ability to break data into neat visual pictures.

Chapter 3.1: Mind Mapping, Map Your Thoughts

Your brain is very different from the computer that's sitting on your desk, although both can store vast amounts of information. The main point of difference is that the computer works in a linear fashion while the brain works in two ways – associatively as well as linearly. The brain can integrate, compare and synthesize all at once - that is the human brain at its efficient best.

This explains one simple thing that we often take for granted. What happens when you hear a word - 'autumn', for instance? Immediately, you see pictures of falling leaves and nippy winds into your mind. If you like drinking hot chocolate, you may even be bombarded by the lingering aroma of chocolate swirls and cozy nightcaps!

In the brain, no single idea exists on its own. Every idea and thought – word even – has many links that attach it to other ideas and concepts. The brain stores information much like **branches on a tree**. There are various related patterns and associations, each forming a new pattern or association of its own as you receive new data. In a nutshell, the human memory is **associative** by nature.

The significance of mind maps is that they ape the brain's storage system. The mind can remember images and keywords easily. It can also make connections and links rapidly. Thus mind maps group associated clumps of information and store data using pictures. Therefore one central idea will trigger a number of associated concepts.

Each map begins with a central theme that branches out into supporting themes and ideas. The branches continue to grow till the entire concept has been depicted pictorially. Thus mind maps strengthen the natural processes of the mind.

If you've ever heard the saying that a single picture is worth a thousand words, you'll immediately understand the effectiveness of using mind maps for learning. Maps help organize data **visually**. Images evoke more memories and associations than words. They are more precise and effective in triggering a wide range of associations.

Mind maps Vs. Traditional learning methods:

As careers start taking off, hundreds of working men and women find themselves put through training sessions – some harrowing and boring, others interesting and colorful. But each equally futile in delivering its full volume of contents to your hapless brain.

Employees who take voluminous notes from their training programs faithfully file these pages of information and promptly forget all about them. Even those who get their books out, sharpen their pencils and tidy up their desks for a day of undisturbed study quickly get distracted and bored. Why does this happen?

This happens because people are still faithful to the old school of linear note-taking and rote-learning.

At this very moment, students all over the world are writing down information line by line or column by column and tediously committing this data to memory. When your brain does not work in nice neat lines, forcing it to learn in a linear fashion will only slow you down. If you try recalling a single line from memory, you'll agree that it is very difficult – if not impossible- to reproduce word to word. Standard notes hamper the learning process.

Standard notes are linear.

Notes obstruct the brain from making associations. Thus information is difficult to remember.

Since notes look boring and monotonous, they put you off.

Notes encourage rote-learning — a time-consuming and mind-numbing task.

Mind maps, on the other hand, stimulate the brain creatively. They encourage the brain to form new associations. By arranging these associations in an attractive manner, they assist easy learning and rapid recall.

Mind maps break down data into manageable groups.

The organization of data in mind maps reflects the way the brain works.

Maps are easy to review. Regular review reinforces memory.

Maps aid visual learning through images and words that stand out and grab attention.

Mind maps clearly show the relationships between main themes, sub-themes, supporting facts and ideas. They form a comprehensive whole that can easily be broken into bits of data.

You have the freedom to add to your maps as you go.

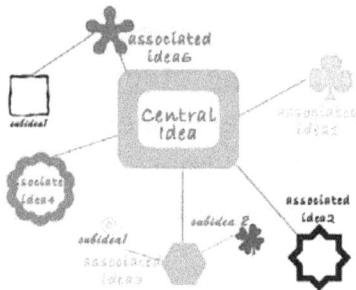

A typical mind map

To be effective, your mind maps should:

Begin with a central image.

Use images lavishly.

Use 3 or more colors for every central image.

Use different sizes of pictures and fonts.

Use white space to organize data.

Associate information using arrows, colors and pictures.

Although mind maps may look strange at first and need a little getting used to, most people who use it find it effective and a lot less work. Once you've mastered the technique of breaking data into associated groups through mind maps, you'll wonder why you ever bothered to read a text book from start to finish!

Chapter 3.1 Recap:

• Accelerated learning techniques improve learning and recall processes by a whopping 70%.

• Visual learning techniques include mind maps, semiotics, linking and chunking.

• Linear learning techniques go against the natural processes of the brain.

• Mind maps break information into groups of associated data thus simulating the mind's natural thought processes.

• In mind maps, a single central idea will automatically trigger all the associated themes and sub-themes.

• Mind maps make data more manageable and enable easy review.

Chapter 3.2: Linking: Learn Faster, Remember More

Learning is a fundamental skill. These days, you need to be sharp when you're in school and sharper still when you're on the job. Your ability to learn dictates your promotion prospects and overall business success.

As retirement ages stretch beyond the horizon, you need an efficient brain for a longer period of time. The only way to ward off age-related mental decline is through good food, proper exercise and continuous efficient learning techniques.

In the years gone by, you'd do pretty well for yourself if you were good at your job, knew any one language well and could make decent communication with your clients. Not any more.

This is the age of power reading, super language skills (a corporate 'SuperBoy' I know speaks six languages and writes four of them) and precise memorization. You must be able to read through a 1,000 word document in less than 3 minutes and come up with its gist (what is called power browsing and will be discussed later). You have to attach names to faces and remember important dates. You must be able to list facts off your finger tips as if you were naming the months of the year and quote last year's projections as if they were written on your palm.

The only way to give yourself that edge is to study and absorb as much as you can while you're on the run (I know an executive who taught himself French during his flights to various parts of Europe). To do that, you must seek out easier and quicker methods of learning.

In short, you should have a **super-chip** in your brain!

How can Linking help learning?

Linking or associating is one of the most effective ways to learn faster and to keep what you have learnt for longer. Imagine how difficult it would be to remember a random list of 9 numbers. But if each of these numbers stood for the number of alphabets in the names of the planets, it would not be difficult any more.

Learning unconnected and unorganized data can be quite challenging. By adding some meaning to the material before learning it, you make it easy to store as well as retrieve information.

As explained earlier, the human brain links ideas and concepts as it receives new data. Each piece of data is linked to another piece and recalling one piece will lead you to all the other pieces of information linked to the first piece. (Remember the effect of the word 'autumn' that we talked about in an earlier chapter?)

Humans naturally remember things through association. For instance, the word 'apple' is linked with a variety of other concepts like 'round', 'red', 'juicy', 'fruit' or 'sweet'. However, it is unlikely that you'd think about milk when you hear the word 'apple' (unless of course you have your apple with a glass of milk).

A person continually makes associations while learning. You make associations between what you are learning, the environment you are in, the different streams of thought in your mind and so on. Most of the times, these associations are unconscious and so they do not help the learning process.

Your memory works faster when you associating things. When ideas and concepts are associated **consciously** in memory, thinking of one idea will automatically retrieve the other concepts linked to it.

The reason we lose a lot of data or have such tough time learning is because we cannot or do not form conscious associations.

For instance, suppose you had to catch a plane at 5, there's nothing about the plane that can remind you of the number '5'. So you forget the plane and work late – only to miss the crucial meeting you were slogging for!

Try this trick: the next time you get an air ticket, notice the time. Suppose your flight is at 3 P.M. Close your eyes and imagine the three wheels of the airplane touching the tarmac. You have formed an association: 'plane=3'. Now you're **10 times** more likely to remember the time of your flight without having to check your ticket manually!

What happened? You formed an association **consciously**. Every time you think about the plane, you see the three wheels and you're reminded of the time.

When there is no obvious relation between pieces of information, we run the risk of losing the information. If you wish to retain it, you have to think creatively and come up with a crucial link.

Here's an example: The French word for poster is l'affiche. Ordinarily, a student would have a difficult time remembering the word. But, you may notice that the word l'affiche sounds like 'LA fish'. Think of a fish from LA stuck to a poster and hammered on to the wall of your kitchen!

"Linking" a mental picture to a word - L'affiche

If you see yourself putting up the poster of a fish from LA, you're more likely to remember the French word than otherwise.

This proves that when we work actively to create an association between 2 pieces of information, we learn faster. The chances for ready recall are 62% higher.

Here's a tip: when you are learning something new, try to associate what you are learning with something you know very well – music, poems, images, rhymes or puns. Chances are that you will never forget what you've learned.

Now you know why they taught you those acronyms in school for ('i' before 'e' except for 'c', **N**ever **E**at **S**our **W**atermelons – for the directions on a compass). These symbols or associations work because they form clever associations that can easily be remembered.

Important points to be remembered while linking seemingly dissimilar items:

• Be creative and clever. The more outlandish the associations, the higher your chances of recall.

• Visualize – after you create the association, close your eyes for a moment and visualize the associated bits of data (like hammering the poster of the fish from LA on to your wall).

• If you have to remember a sequence, create a jingle out of the associations and string them together (**M**y **V**ery **E**ducated **M**other **J**ust **S**aw **U**s **N**odding – for the planets in our solar system)

Will you clutter your brain with all those nonsensical links and associations you're thinking up?

Since your brain can store limitless amounts of data, there's little chance of cluttering it up. On the other hand, when you have associated something many times, you begin to remember the sequence **minus** the association (meaning you'll soon learn that the word for fish is l'affiche and you won't need the poster any more). So, you're freeing that sector of your brain.

You can use associations to fix names to faces, remember your list of groceries, learn and remember the points in an important section of your training manual or fix your friend's phone number permanently in your mind.

At first, linking may seem a silly exercise (How **could** you think such a harebrained thing – and at your age too!!), but with time, this method will become second nature to you. Once you taste the ease with which you learn and experience the error-free method of rapid recall, you will never want to let go of the funny side of things – purely for study purposes of course!

Chapter 3.2 Recap:

• The brain remembers through associations.

• To learn faster, we have to actively create associations between seemingly unrelated ideas or concepts.

• Linking or associating becomes effective when it follows certain principles.

• Associations become strongly embedded in the mind when they are visualized.

• After a period of use, associations are naturally discarded by the brain, which picks up related concepts without the help of supporting associations.

Chapter 3.3: Chunking, The Art Of Eating An Elephant.

How do you eat an Elephant? One bite at time... In other words break it down into manageable chunks.

Here's a list:

Cabbage, Beans, Carrots, Kiwi, Cauliflower, Oranges, Apples, Bananas, Cherries, Tomatoes and Pears

Now, try to remember this list without missing out a single thing. Your wife wants those items in the fridge in one hour – so you haven't all afternoon to memorize.

Going round in circles? That's not your fault really.

Way back in 1952, George Miller put forward the idea that the conscious memory can cope with 7 items of information only at one time, give or take one or two. That means that 7 is the magic number; you can hold between 5 and 9 pieces of information at one time. That's why most countries have 6 or 7 digits in their local phone numbers and pin codes.

But what if you had to learn your social security number?

If you have to remember more than 7-9 items, you're in trouble. Obviously, there'd be a memory overflow and you'd lose data that went beyond the pail of your memory's capacity. UNLESS, you could find a way to keep it all in.

Chunking:

We practice chunking instinctively when we try to learn a new phone number. It can be observed in the way we group numbers in our daily life without quite realizing it.

For instance, look at this number: **15301955**. In itself, this number looks quite formidable, but if that's an important number you automatically look for a work around: **15 30 1955**. The first chunk is 15, and the second chunk is twice the first: 30. The third chunk is for the year 1955 – perhaps it was the year a favorite aunt was born. Look at it that way and the number is already printed into your brain.

Chunking is a process of learning that allows you to split data into manageable chunks. Even while chunking, the rule of 5-9 items hold true. But when you chunk data, you decrease the number of items you hold in memory by increasing the size of each chunk.

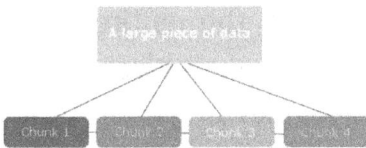

Chunking

Chunking is a little like cutting pieces of food into bite-sized morsels so you can eat all the food that's on your plate. It makes use of categorization to classify information into different groups. Ordering data efficiently into groups makes it easier to learn. Therefore, chunking is a flexible way of learning.

These kinds of systems existed even before Miller discovered the magic of the number '7'. But conscious application of this general strategy became possible after Miller. Today, almost all kinds of memory training systems include some amount of drill and training in chunking schemes.

Now, let's get back to the list we had earlier on and group the items like so:

Cabbage, Carrots, Cauliflower, **Beans, Tomatoes,** Apples, Bananas, Cherries, Kiwi, Oranges, Pears

We first break the entire list into two broad groups: vegetables and fruits. The first three veggies begin with the alphabet 'C'; and the first three fruits begin with 'A', 'B' and 'C'.

Try the list again. Easier this time?

Chunking is most effective when the order of items is not important. It is particularly well suited for learning and memorizing multi-digit numbers and for remembering complicated spellings. Once data is broken into chunks, they can then be learned by rote.

When should you use chunking?

• When you have data that can be broken into pieces.

• When the details of the data seem to be overwhelming, chunk up to find the bigger picture, so you can make sense of the smaller details.

• When you want to learn a long speech, chunk it down into slices of meaningful pieces and link various pieces together.

How do you chunk up to find the bigger picture?

Asking certain questions can help:
• Is this a part of the whole? If so, what is it a part of?
• Is this the example of a class?
• What is the outcome of this chunk?
• What is the purpose?
To chunk down, you may have to ask:
• What is the bigger picture?
• Is there an example of the class?
• How can you piece data to achieve the outcome?
• Is there any other piece of information that can satisfy the same set of principles?
Learning and retention become easy if you can find a way to link or associate various chunks of data. Using chunking with linking or associating can become a handy and powerful tool for accelerated learning. On the one hand, chunking makes it easy to break data down into small sizes; on the other, associating these chunks helps string together pieces of data. Now you have manageable groups of data that can easily be recalled.

Like any other memory technique, chunking also requires some amount of practice. Trying to break huge amounts of information into logical pieces of data is a habit; looking for relationships between these pieces becomes second nature after some practice with linking. Regular review of chunks and links is important to transfer data from short-term memory to long-term memory.

Chapter 3.3 Recap:
• We practice chunking in our day to day life without being conscious of what we are   doing.
• Chunking is breaking up larger pieces of data into smaller manageable groups.
• Chunking is particularly useful with numbers   and   lists.
• Depending on the information you need to learn, you can chunk up or chunk down.
• Chunking becomes even more effective when it is used in tandem with association or linking.

Chapter 11: Learning and Mastering New Skills Fast

It is one thing to memorize the name of someone and a completely different thing to learn and master a new skill. In your student and professional life, you will encounter many instances when you will need to learn and master a new skill so you can become an expert. Apart from that, you often develop a certain likeness towards a subject or an area that compels you to develop a certain skill. For all those times when you must become skilled in something, try the following strategies.

Have a Compelling Goal

Learning something for the sake of learning something new hardly lasts. If you truly want to build a skill and master it, it is best to peg it to a specific, compelling goal that motivates you to work on that skill and become adept at it.

For instance, if you want to learn French, you are likely to lose interest in this idea if you just focus on learning a new language. However, if you set a goal to learn French so you can impress your French employer so that he hires you into his fashion design company that you would love to work at, you are likely to feel more interested in acquiring that skill and becoming seasoned at it.

When setting a goal, identify the big reason behind it that motivates you towards it. Why are you interested in learning this skill? What will you gain if you build that skill? How will acquiring that skill change your life for the better? Figure out your whys for working on a skill and use them to compel yourself to work on it so your motivation for it never dies.

Chop It

You cannot become an expert overnight: a lot of hard work, patience, and time goes into becoming an expert. When you think of the huge amount of effort you would need to put into learning a skill, doing so will naturally become overwhelming for you and you are likely to quit that pursuit. To keep things easy for yourself and to ensure you do not become emotionally overwhelmed when trying to master a skill, break it into smaller, easy-to-do parts.

For instance, if you are trying to learn French, break this task into parts such as: learn to count in French, learn how to greet in French, learn commonly used French words, and develop the ability to form short sentences after 1 month of working on French. When you chop a difficult skill into smaller parts, things suddenly seem more doable and your enthusiasm to build that skill increases.

Try and Practice

After identifying the smaller steps you need to work your way through to acquire and master a certain skill, your job is to actually execute those steps and then practice them repeatedly until you perfect them. Famous martial art expert, actor, director, and philosopher Bruce Lee once said,

"I fear not the man who has practiced 10, 000 kicks once, but I fear the man who has practiced one kick 10, 000 times.'

This beautiful quote by Bruce Lee shows that if you practice something repeatedly, you become an expert at it and once you become an expert at something, you are likely to beat amateurs. Therefore, practice everything you want to master and make sure you work on your weaknesses so you overcome them and refine your strengths.

Chapter 12: Practical Ways for Increasing

Brain Power

Having a strong memory is really dependent on the vitality and health of one's brain. It does not matter if you are a student, a professional, or a person in his advanced years. There are suitable and practical routines that you can follow in order to improve your mental capability. In this chapter, it will be shown how you can harness your brain power.

An ancient axiom tells us that new tricks can't be learned by old dogs. But scientists tell us differently. The brains of human beings have an amazingly high level of flexibility and susceptibility to alteration. Even when a person is already old, he can still learn a lot. This ability is summarized by one term: neuroplasticity. With the correct method of stimulating your brain, it can create new pathways for neurons. This changes connections that exist in the network of neurons. In effect, the brain reacts and adapts in ways that are ever-changing.

Here are some practical and incredible ways to increase your brain power. Unleash the inner genius by doing the following:

Do jumping jacks on a regular basis. Aside from reading books and studying hard, you can resort to jumping jacks and other aerobic activities to make you more intellectual. This is explained by the fact that exercise can increase the level of oxygen in our brain. Also, physical activities can reduce the risk of having loss of memory and other brain disorders. Other benefits include the prevention of cardiovascular disease and diabetes. Most significantly, the exercise can produce brain chemicals that can aid in protecting the neurons.

While you do any kind of physical workout, listen to music. It does not matter what genre – be it classic, meditational/healing, or even Lady Gaga. Studies recommend that any kind of music can help you increase your cognitive skills.

Do some strength training. By hitting the weight room frequently, you will be able to bulk up your brain. Such activity can increase the levels of BDNF (brain-derived neurotrophic factor) or brain develop neurotrophic factor vividly. This chemical has a direct control on the growth and increase of the nerves.

Do some power naps. Aside from the usual good night's sleep, you should also engage in some power naps. According to study, 90-minute power nap can increase the memory.

Get more prepared. Establishing your workspace, studies show, proves to be helpful in improving cognitive skills and memory.

Doodle a lot. Doodling, an activity you were fond of when you were a kid, turns out to be an effective brain stimulus activity.

Floss your teeth. It does not only keep your teeth and gums in their tiptop shape. Flossing also removes the plaque. Do you know that plaque prevents nutrients from reaching your brain? If you want those essential nutrients to reach your control panel, floss regularly!

Do the lawn mowing chore. Yes, many people consider it as a chore. But do you know that it can release chemical compounds that help you relieve the stress? In the long run, it can boost your memory, too.

Have sex every day. If you are an adult, engaging in sexual activities on a daily basis will aid you because it can increase your creativity, logic, and decision-making skills, according to the American Psychological Association. This is because the oxytocin hormone can only be released by having a sexual interaction. This hormone's effect on our conduct and physiology makes in the brain, it is formed by the by an arrangement called the hypothalamus, and then transfers to the pituitary gland which releases into the blood... Oxytocin receptors are found on cells through the body like antennas picking up a signal, during both stressful and socially bonding experiences the Levels of the hormone tend to be higher

Think about your origins. Brain power can greatly increase if you will try to explore who your ancestors are. Knowing your roots does not only increase your memory and boost your IQ, it also increases your sense of control.

Meditate regularly. Remove your worries and anxiety by doing meditation. A mind that's full of worries cannot think clearly – that's a fact. Not only that, meditation improves your concentration skills, your capability to create sound decisions, your attention span, and your memory. In addition to that, it helps heal you from within.

Play video games regularly. Try hanging out with your friends and play your favorite game. Aside from improving your relationship with them, playing Xbox game will also improve your capability to multitask, your skills related to spatial cognition, and your other cognitive skills. And it is also super cool, you are actually persuaded that you are getting smart by just doing it.

In moderation, watch television. Yes, it is not that terrible. It won't make you dumb if it's not the only thing you do the whole day. Watching the television for half an hour every day will help you increase your IQ. It is equal to listening to Mozart's compositions, working on Sudoku, and reading books.

Lie down. This increases your posture. If you can, hang upside down like a monkey because it increases memory. If you can't the next best substitute is by lying down.

CHAPTER 13: Debunking Speed Reading

Myths

Speed reading has its own share of myths surrounding it. You yourself may have harboured some of these preconceived ideas. It's important that you are fully aware of these myths if you are really serious in learning the art of speed reading. Let's take a closer look into some of these myths.

1. That you don't enjoy reading as much if you speed read. This is without a doubt the biggest criticism often lobbed against practitioners of speed reading. However, it's not true. Speed reading only increases your speed in consuming textual content. It doesn't take away the joy of reading. Contrary to the myth, speed reading is all about efficient reading. In fact, for a lot of people who speed read, their enjoyment from reading increases twofold or even threefold because they get to read more content. It's more enjoyable to read two

books instead of just one book within the same timeframe.

2. That you don't comprehend as well when you speed read. It's really strange that people tend to associate speed reading with decreased comprehension skills when there's no evidence to prove such claim. The truth is that speed reading actually helps with your comprehension skills because it trains your brain to process information with more speed and better efficiency. What's more, by reading several words or phrases at the same time rather than one word after the other increases your comprehension skills.

3. That you are a better reader if you read every letter. Many people have the mistaken assumption that good readers read each letter in a word in order to fully comprehend what is being discussed. Quite the contrary if you are to learn about how the brain works. The brain can easily decode and comprehend the message in a text without taking in every letter and every word. This is because the human brain is naturally wired to look for

the meaning of what is being read rather than concern itself with the exact letter placement of words and phrases. Good comprehension is still highly possible without processing every letter and word in your head.

4. That you can't concentrate if you are speed reading. People always assume that it is going to be difficult to concentrate if you are speed reading. That is not the case at all. Another variation of this myth is the claim that you will better understand what you are reading if you read slowly. In some ways, there are some truth to this but it's not absolute. In fact, there are some people who tend to experience demotion in their comprehension skills if they read slowly. Here's what you need to understand: speed reading isn't just about reading faster. It's also about training yourself to be able to concentrate while you read faster. The two come hand in hand. In other words, if you are speed reading right, not only are you reading faster, you are also concentrating better.

5. That speed reading is very difficult to learn. Speed reading is a skill. And just like any skill, it takes time for anyone to learn it. Individual progress in learning the skill also varies. Some people will learn faster and some people will learn much slower. Let's just say that if you are new into speed reading, there are many challenges that you are going to go through. But this doesn't mean that the learning process is difficult. It takes time. It takes patience. And yes, it takes a lot of practice. Is it difficult? No. Speed reading gets easier and easier as you practice. There will come a time when the process comes at you naturally. You will be speed reading through articles and books without you even fully aware of it.

6. That speed reading causes stress and anxiety. There's absolutely no evidence to prove that this is true. No research, no data, nothing. This myth is usually propagated by people who either have never tried speed reading or they have tried but gave up on their first or second try. The truth is that there is no

connection between speed reading and stress or anxiety. In fact, for many speed readers, speed reading helps them deal with stress and anxiety. They get to enjoy more books and content in less time. That in itself is a great thing. For a lot of people, reading is a form of therapy. All speed reading does is help increase the therapeutic effects of reading.

7. That it's too late to learn speed reading if you are already an adult. Remember that old saying that goes: "Old cows don't learn." Well, that saying doesn't apply to speed reading. Speed reading isn't a skill that only the young folks can learn to do. As long as you can read, you can pick up speed reading. It doesn't matter if you are eight years old or eighty years old. It is never too late to learn speed reading. What's great about it is that you can practice it anywhere and anytime. Just pick up a book or browse through an ebook in your smartphone and you can practice for as long as you want.

8. That speed reading is next to useless in the digital age. It's quite the contrary if

you truly think about it. In fact, the skill of speed reading is even more important today than it was twenty years ago since the internet started to revolutionize the way people access and consume content. Today, we are being bombarded with tons and tons of new content every single day. When we look into our Facebook newsfeed; when we check in our email messages; when we visit our favorite blogs. There's just too much content that we can't go through all of them even if we want to. Fortunately, with the help of speed reading, at least we have the chance of getting to the content that are of the most importance to us.

As we have learned in this chapter, there's a lot of myths and misconceptions about speed reading out there. It's important that you are aware of these myths so that you won't fall into their traps. It will be more difficult for you to learn the skill of speed reading if you still harbor some of these myths and misconceptions.

Chapter 14: Laser Focus

The human attention span has taken a serious hit with the increasing prevalence of technology. In fact, in 2013, Microsoft did a study that revealed that since 2000 (the dawn of mobile technology), the human attention span decreased from 12 seconds to eight seconds – one second less than the average goldfish.

You can probably imagine what a drop like that has done to our ability to learn. A lack of focus makes it extremely difficult to understand and retain new information.
The Things that Prevent Focus

Our ability to focus is tested constantly. We battle distractions both real and digital. Here are some of the things that pose the biggest threat to our ability to focus:

☐Devices, particularly mobile devices, are a huge distraction in the modern world. When was the last time you had a conversation with somebody who wasn't distracted by the beeping of their phone? Unfortunately, such distractions have become a way of life.

☐Our thoughts also have the potential to distract us. When your mind wanders and you think about a mistake you made yesterday or a worry you have about tomorrow, you're not in the present moment – and that impedes your ability to learn.

☐ Finally, the brutal truth is that our society does not place a premium on the ability to focus. We flit from subject to subject, and from thought to thought, with little consideration for what it does to our brains.

Unfortunately, it can be virtually impossible to avoid distractions. That's not the end of the world – provided that you can learn how to ignore them when you need to.

The Dangers of Multitasking

Multitasking is something we brag about doing. It used to be that doing one thing at a time, and doing it well, was considered a virtue. Today, we hardly feel adequate if we're not trying to do five things at once.

However, the truth is that multitasking is code for dividing our attention. We can't excel at any one thing because we're doing a sub-par job on five things that we're attempting to do at the same time.

To get an idea of how much time you can waste attempting to multitask, try this simple exercise. Get a stopwatch, a piece of paper, and a pen. On the first line, write "Good morning" one letter at a time. Alternate that task with writing the numbers one through 10 on the second line – and time yourself doing it.

Then, repeat the task by simply doing one task first and then the other. Write "Good morning" and then write the letters one through 10 below it. What you'll notice is that it takes you significantly less time to do the tasks sequentially than it does to try to do them both at once.

It's a simple example, but it illustrates the problem with multitasking. You'll perform more quickly, accurately, and efficiently if you do one thing at a time.

Tips for Eliminating Distractions

The key to focusing on what you need to do is to find way to eliminate distractions. Here are some suggestions:

Put your mobile device away and check it at predetermined intervals instead of responding to everything at once.

Turn notifications off on your computer and check emails at specific times of day.

Play classical music, which can improve focus, while you study.

Have a dedicated study area with no television and with a minimum of distractions.

It may also help you to identify those things that most frequently distract you so you can learn to avoid them as needed.

The Pomodoro Technique

One focusing technique that can be very helpful is the Pomodoro Technique. First discovered by Italian researcher Francesco Cirillo. He used a tomato-shaped timer to manage his time, hence the name "pomodoro," which means tomato in Italian.

The technique is easy. Simply set a timer or an alarm for 25 minutes. Remove all distractions and tell yourself that you will focus intently on one task until the timer goes off.

When it does, take a quick, five-minute break and then reset the timer. This technique helps you work with time instead of against it. Focusing for hours at a time is difficult, but working in short bursts of energy helps keep your

brain fresh – particularly if you take a quick five-minute walk between sessions.

Next up, we'll talk about a problem that often goes hand-in-hand with a lack of focus: procrastination. If you struggle with procrastination, then the next chapter will help you banish it for good.

Chapter 15: What it Means to Have Self-Discipline (and Why it Matters)

When the average person considers the word "discipline," they may have mixed feelings. For many, "discipline" might conjure up a childhood memory where, because they may have disobeyed or done something bad, they were forced to endure a spanking, a loss of TV privileges, or even freedom itself – the right being revoked by an irate parent who says something along the lines of, "You're grounded."

It's a shame that for so many people, discipline is considered as something unpleasant, given that the word itself is so closely connected with "punishment." And while it is true that a parent may punish their child to discipline them, in reality, the word discipline comes from the Latin word "disciplina" which means "instruction" and/or "knowledge". At its core, that's all discipline is: instruction and knowledge being imparted to a person so that they might behave in a certain way.

Yes, this is something that is absolutely necessary for a child whose minimal understanding of reality requires that they must be taught the "correct" ways in which to behave. But for those who have left the nest or are close to doing so – adults, young adults, and even teenagers – learning how to discipline oneself is crucial for building independence, healthy habits, and, of course, achieving one's pined for goals.

And that, to put it simply, is all self-discipline really is: giving yourself instruction and knowledge to control your life the way you wish.

Now you may be asking: isn't self-discipline something everyone does 24/7? Doesn't every decision of a mentally competent adult bring with it self-discipline since the decision itself is being made and carried out by the person?

The answers to these questions are yes and no. And this is because there are actually two types of self-discipline: active and passive.

As an example, say there are two people. Jim and Jack. Both of them hold down steady jobs; but, while Jim prefers to live his life with no sort of plan – just trying to get by while taking things day by day – Jack likes to set goals for himself – long and short term – and tries to make a concentrated effort to better his life.

It is between these two figures that you can see the clear difference. Yes, Jim does have a small amount of passive self-discipline that allows him to set his alarm clock and get up in the morning so that he can make it to work and won't end up in the unemployment line, but unlike Jack, he won't start to see any real improvements in his life unless he starts to practice active discipline.

But before we get into all that, let's take a step back and look a little closer at what self-discipline is.

First and foremost, it is important to realize that self-discipline isn't something that is given to you. Sure, you might have some residual discipline imparted to you by your parents, and you can research some particular ways that will help you become more disciplined (actually, you're doing that right now by reading this book) but overall, it is something that comes from within you. It is the offspring of your desire to better yourself and your willingness to shape your actions around that desire. Therefore, it can be said that self-discipline is a product of your willpower because, through sheer force of will, you can start to change your experience.

As for self-discipline and willpower's ultimate purpose, there are many differing opinions. Biology would take the stance of "survival of the fittest" where those with the strongest will and self-discipline to live had the best chance of mating and reproducing offspring. Philosophers, such as Friedrich Nietzsche, claimed that the will to power (i.e. achievement, ambition, and trying to reach the highest possible position in one's life) was the main driving force in human beings.

While a conclusive answer to why self-discipline exists may never be fully revealed, there have been numerous conclusions in the school of psychology that may help to explain where the particular ability comes from in humans. One of the main psychological theories concerning self-discipline and willpower is **"The Energy Model of Self- Control.**"

According to this theory, the inner workings of the human brain behave like a muscle that is being exercised when a person is exerting willpower and self-control. The theory also posits that similar to a more familiar muscle like a bicep, there is only so much energy available for the brain to use to produce self-discipline. So for example, when a person practices self-control by forcing themselves to study for an extended period, or by stopping themselves from eating that second piece of cake, they are using a limited amount of brain power for self-discipline. The theory goes on to say that once this limited amount of brain power is depleted, the person might have a very difficult time practicing self-discipline and willpower unless they give their mental task a break so that the brain can recharge.

It is here that opinions split, however. Some proponents of this theory think that it is possible to replenish the brain's power to exert self-discipline by refueling it (literally) with carbohydrates – again, like an arm muscle. But there are others who see the actual act of self-discipline as a means of achieving more brain power to do it. That is, they believe that the brain can become stronger the more a person practices self-discipline, meaning the more you practice self-discipline, the better at it you will become!

Whether or not this theory is true, it would be hard to deny that the more one practices self-discipline, the easier it tends to get. And this brings us to our first big lesson: the benefits of self-discipline.

So far we've touched on some of the reasons why we might have self-discipline, and also the reason how the brain allows us to exert it. But still, one question remains: what are the specific, beneficial results?

Now, since every human being have a different set of goals for his or her life, what they hope to achieve by way of self-discipline vary from person to person. But, if practiced correctly, self-discipline can aid everybody in attaining the same advantageous thing: good habits.

When you think about it, our lives revolve around habits more than we might like to admit. What we like to eat, the things we like to do and say, and even the ways in which our minds think can oftentimes be nothing more than a simple habit. Of course, there are bad and good habits, but by practicing active self-discipline, you are far more likely to do away with those in the former category and build up a strong repertoire of those in the latter one.

In a way, good habits and self-discipline are like a reinforcing feedback loop. You can't have one without the other and each of them makes the other stronger. Whatever it is you want to do with your life, whatever outcome it is you want from your particular efforts, 9 times out of 10 that ideal thing can only be got because you cultivated good habits by way of self-discipline to get it.

And so to reiterate, that right there is why self-discipline matters: not because it is given to you by someone else, but because it is given to you by you. No one can tell you to become fitter, happier, or wealthier; you need to take the steps to do those things on their own, and by actively utilizing self-discipline and willpower, you are already operating light-years ahead of others who would rather just sit around and wait for these things to fall down into their laps.

Since you're reading this, it's safe to say that you've already made the initial effort to begin down the road to self-discipline. Later, I'll get into why the first step of every journey, while very important, can sometimes be misleading because we tend to underestimate how long the metaphorical journey will take – which sometimes lead to discouragement. Luckily, you only have to make it through five chapters here where, at the end of which, you will have hopefully built up an arsenal of positive habits that will help to change your life and – once they see the monumental leaps you've taken by way of self-discipline – potentially the lives of those who know you as well.

In the following chapters, we will be looking at specific beneficial habits of self-disciplined people, and how the implementation of these particular habits can help you in your quest for self-improvement!

Chapter 16: Developing a Successful Mindset

If you want to be successful in anything you do, your biggest priority needs to be working on developing and maintaining an affirmative attitude. When you have optimism working for you, your opportunities grow, and problems shrink.

Live each day with a sense of purpose

Decide on what your goals in life are before acting on them. This helps to better serve your goals positively. If an action doesn't strongly connect with your line of goals, then you should take it off the list and move on to things that are more productive for you. Acting aimlessly only wastes precious energy and time.

Expand your personal boundaries

Doing the same things day in and day out, despite your success with them in the past, is only going to keep you within the constraints of your comfort zone. Look at succeeding like being an athlete; if you don't stretch every single day, you will slowly become slow and unable to beat new records.

Stop expecting results and just do it

While it is natural to act based on decisions that lean on the results we may receive, you should stray away from this habit. When you do this, you are much more likely to be easily disappointed. Do your best and take the best crack at things, but don't obsess over your target.

Utilize setbacks and weaknesses to improve yourself further

Instead of feeling negative about failure and rejection, take a glance back at the actions you did. Instead, look at what you can do rather than what you cannot do at this time. The results you get are further signs of what you eventually desire to achieve.

Spend time with like-minded people

Your brain is wired to imitate the behaviors of the people you surround yourself with. If you are always hanging around negative people, you are likely to become negative and see your world in a dark sense. Do your best to spend your time around positive people.

Be Funnier

If you want to be happier, you need to make yourself laugh more often. Look at funny photos. Tell funny jokes and make others laugh. Spend time with your kids and perform funny faces. Nothing is as addicting as the laugh of a child. There are many things that you can do to cultivate laughter!

Forgive others' weaknesses

It is essential to always remember that every single person out there is human, just like you. Stop making yourself miserable because other people can't do a job as well as you think you could. If you are more passionate about something and find that others don't quite share your vision, do your best to help them see the positivity you see. That is all you can do.

Tell others 'thank you' frequently

Achieving a great attitude of gratitude requires more than being aware of all the wonderful aspects of your life. You should always go out of your way to thanks others in your life for the gifts of their presence they bless you with, even if it is as simplistic as a smile.

You are the CEO of your attitude

Attitude does not emerge from what happens to you, but instead from how you decide to interpret what happens to you.

Believe positively

Your beliefs rule your life and help decide how you interpret the world. Therefore, you need to adopt strong beliefs that help cultivate a better attitude rather than the opposite.

Develop a large array of positive affirmations

I personally spend 15-minutes every morning either listening, looking at, or reading motivational and/or inspirational things. When you do this on a regular basis, you naturally have those thoughts and feelings around with you throughout the day. They become especially handy when things don't go as you planned.

Don't get sucked into social media

The majority of media these days is loaded full of hateful people. When you expose yourself constantly to social media, it slowly destroys your ability to cultivate a positive attitude. In fact, media has been proven by science to place you in a state of misery. Limit your consumptions of media.

Ignore complainers

Whiners see the world through entirely different spectacles than positive folks. They'd rather talk about what's wrong rather than make things better. Complainers can't bear to see others happy.

Use positive terms

The words that come out of your mouth are a direct reflection of what you are thinking. They are powerful enough to program your mind how to think. If you want to have a better attitude, your vocabulary must be consistently positive.

Easy Steps to Implement a Positive Attitude

Tell yourself that you can change

Happiness is not just a belief. Take a moment to recognize the correspondence between personal growth and change.

Try writing down at least 3 great moments in your life that changed you. They can be milestones, or they can be simplistic. Hang that list where you can see it so that you naturally adapt to staying more positive.

Go somewhere else

It is easy to blow even small negativities way out of proportion when you are stressed and overworked. New environments, however, can completely change your perspective.

Try exposing your mind to a new place. Either go somewhere else or read in a new spot to help you gain a change in your attitude.

Re-energize

When you are tired and hungry, this is a bad combination that can damage your train of thought. Your brain is trained to see a lack of sleep as a physical threat to your nervous system. When you are well-rested and fed, it is much easier to see details, information, and possibilities.

Try looking at your sleeping and eating habits if you find that you are cranky a lot of the time. Eat healthy snacks and get adequate sleep.

Identify the positive and the negative

No matter how bad a situation, there is always a silver lining lying around the corner. You will never encounter an experience where there are no positive things to be found.

Try focusing on just one task and list as many things as you can for 30 seconds. List three positive and one negative descriptor. Ensure you include that negative. It may seem counterproductive, but it motivates you to act and look at them more flexibly.

Speak with the right folks

Venting to others about the negativities in your life can do more harm than good. When you speak with like-minded people, this discourages problem-solving. If you want a positive attitude, you need to seek out various points of view.

Try using a reality check from a three-person point of view. This will help you cover all your bases:

Find someone with a different personality

Find someone with a different economic status

Find someone of a different age group

Channel your stress effectively

Stress has the power to make any situation worse, even those that are not so bad.

Try channeling your stress differently. If you are worried about something, such as a presentation at work, it is likely just the stress you have about impressing the big man, not speaking in front of an audience. Direct your stress into a better delivery!

Chapter 17: Memory Enhancement

Through Memory Supplements

While due significance is given to wellness and even muscle growth, many individuals will, in general, overlook the importance of memory improvement. Hugely your age expands, the job of supplements likewise increments. Very few individuals know that our cerebrum is additionally a muscle and this muscle works more diligently than many different tissues.

It is a legend that our psyche is working just when we are thinking. However, the reality remains that our brain is always working and needs to upgrade too. With age, our mind which is continually handling something or the other undertaking feels the absence of sustenance or upgrade.

The ideal approach to help the most significant muscle of our body is to go for memory enhancing supplements which have painstakingly picked herbs as their primary fixing. Improving your mind will, in the end, help you increment the personal satisfaction. As supplements are natural, they help us from various perspectives.

Points of interest of Memory Enhancements

Memory helps you through the procedure of memory improvement.

You would fundamentally recall your undertakings, which will help you in your profitability.

You will achieve your undertakings in a promising way, which is the best practice utilized towards satisfying your objectives.

You can plan better once your mind works adequately.

Your presentation relies upon your psychological exhibition, so in that manner, supplements would, in the end, increment your general execution.

Many individuals have affirmed that supplements make you increasingly sure about whatever you do.

Not just do memory supplements support memory. However, they help vitality too.

In the end, a sound personality will decrease your pressure.

A sound life spins around a stable personality, so memory enhancing supplements merit each penny. Memory supplements help you keep up an audio mind, so your methodology towards doing things will change. With everything taken into account, a memory upgrade is an all-encompassing rendition of wellness.

Purchasing memory supplements should be possible through stores and online gateways. Go for a memory supplement manufacturing organization which is known for its quality. Purchasing on the web can get you many limits and offers yet ensure you don't bargain quality in the can foresee aggressive rates.

To total everything, all-encompassing memory upgrade encourages you to be hopeful about existence as it helps the most significant muscle of your body, which stays at work longer than required - our psyche. Supplements are exceptionally suggested for every last one for a stable personality which would enable you to crest your psychological exhibition.

Memory Enhancers - Go For the Natural and Practical Ways

I'm sure you have all viewed The Notebook, a story by Nicholas Sparks which portrayed the beginning of dementia or memory misfortune in individuals. This undermining sickness is for the most part hereditary however when you are not cautious enough with how you deal with yourself, your way of life, the sustenance that you eat, you may very well be a contender for early memory misfortune, Alzheimer's or dementia.

There are currently different items and administrations, called memory enhancers, that can help forestall this sort of disease. There are prescriptions just as typical memory enhancers that you can take to make your mind more advantageous and progressively dynamic. It will likewise support you if you realize what you are managing. So we should set aside some effort to talk about what memory is and what are the things to can do to deal with it.

With the goal for you to think about the significance of memory enhancers, you ought to see first what it serves - your memory. One of the psychological abilities that our brains have is a memory. Much the same as some other ability, you can either be great at it or awful at it. We should analyze memory into two sections: You have the long haul and the present moment.

By temperance of its definition, transient memory does not keep going long. At a given period, it can just take around 5-7 lumps of data at any given moment, and after that, it is overlooked. The primary way that these pieces of data can go to your long haul memory is if you continue getting to them through consistent review or retention. Furthermore, at this day and age when individuals are assaulted with a large number of information every moment, it is no big surprise that individuals don't just will, in general, have a lack of ability to concentrate consistently issue yet also low memory limit.

Along these lines, the accompanying memory enhancers can enable you to expand your memory as well as your general cerebrum working too.

Down to earth memory enhancers incorporate centering at one undertaking at any given moment. Many of us like to perform various tasks, which is reasonable. In any case, if you need to improve your psychological capacities, at that point, pursue this trip, which is extraordinary compared to other memory enhancers you can take for yourself. Thus, listening admirably, rehashing in your very own words what you have tuned in to and assessing the things you're found out right now, for instance, are likewise extraordinary memory enhancers that you can rehearse. Moreover, you can apply the utilization of abbreviations or memory aids. Furthermore, ultimately, practice usually and eat a decent eating routine. This will cultivate generally speaking great wellbeing, and better cerebrum working.

You don't generally require manufactured disposition enhancers except if you are one of those the weakening ailment. By rehearsing these straightforward memory enhancers, you will be en route to dementia and Alzheimer's free sundown years.

What Is The Best Memory Enhancer For You

The issue with discovering what is 'ideal' for a specific individual is the way that what might be the 'best' for you may not be the best for another person. Truth be told, by and large, what is the best for many, individuals can end up being the most exceedingly awful conceivable alternative for many others. When making sense of what is the 'best' answer for memory improvement, we need to recall that there is no such thing as a 'cutout' arrangement. Various individuals from many multiple foundations have diverse everyday schedules and have numerous issues influencing them. Making sense of the best memory upgrade routine or item for these people must perceive their one of a kind circumstances and conditions. By tending to emotional contrasts and considering in the particular terms and details for every individual, we can discover what is 'ideal' for them. This is the main reasonable answer for deciding the 'best' arrangement, particularly with regards to something as fragile and touchy as memory work. Remember the accompanying tips when searching for a memory enhancer that best accommodates your specific circumstance. Make sense of your degree of memory weakening.

When attempting to unravel memory corruption, you would prefer not to place yourself in a circumstance where you are taking out ants with a flamethrower. There is no compelling reason to spend heaps of cash, time, and exertion on mind boosting upgrades when you need a little assistance. Also, you would prefer not to place yourself in a circumstance where you're attempting to put out a flame by tossing thimbles brimming with water at the blazes either. To keep away from either situation, you need a genuine appraisal of your memory state. How awful are your memory issues? How regularly do you overlook things? Do you forget things so much that it hinders your life happiness or might expose you to conceivable mischief or security dangers? Make sense of how awful your circumstance is before thinking about potential arrangements.

Begin low and moderate

When you have made sense of the degree of your memory weakening, you have to begin moderate. Begin actualizing memory-boosting regimens and check whether there is any improvement. When you see improvement, proceed with the present degree of memory-boosting exercises. If not, you have to slope things up until you see some improvement. If you achieve a point where you feel that you have done everything you could do on an individual premise, you may need to see your doctor for expert mediation. Now, medicine and conceivable office care may be all together. In any case, when attempting to address your memory issues, it is a smart thought to begin low and begin moderate. Once more, you would prefer not to place yourself in a circumstance where you blow up and shoot away at your issues when for reasons unknown, a milder and continuous methodology would have carried out the responsibility.

Begin with the way of life

A ton of memory disintegration has to do with way of life. If you live an inactive and recluse like way of life, your odds of creating memory misfortune or corruption issues is higher than if you carry on with a genuinely dynamic way of life and you continually practice your relational abilities. Be progressively active. Run or stroll around the square. Welcome your neighbors and exercise your capacity to interface faces with names. Keep in mind a couple of subtleties for each look you meet. Attempt to get more rest. Lack of sleep smothers mind work. Ensure you get eight hours of continuous rest during the evening. You might need to practice twice

162

during the day toward the beginning of the day, and at night, so you can be worn out enough to rest right as the night progressed. Watch what you eat. Eat a more beneficial low-fat high-fiber diet to support your cardiovascular wellbeing. Your mind is very oxygen hungry, and it requires ideal bloodstream levels. Offer this to your account by watching what you eat and practicing right. Way of life is the best memory enhancer accessible.

Use nourishment supplements

The Chinese have utilized gingko Biloba for a long time for memory improvement. There are different supplements available which help memory and review abilities. Attempt these nourishment supplements to help support your general bloodstream.

How to Improve Memory and Recall

Retaining data is performed in three stages. As a matter of first importance, individuals see the data just because. Next, they attempt to become familiar with new thoughts. The last advance is called reviewing. It includes acquiring mind the ideas that have been learned previously. When one of these means is performed with trouble, individuals experience memory issue. To discover how to improve memory and review, it is a great idea to gain proficiency with specific methods.

Mental helpers speak to methods that help individuals to improve memory and review by acknowledging associations between the thoughts that must be educated. Above all else, arranging things and getting ready records will help individuals to enhance memory and analysis fundamentally. Learning many ideas that are not identified with one another is troublesome. This is the reason it is a great idea to acknowledge associations between the thoughts.

Learning the request of the components in a single rundown is an approach too this. A comparable technique, which is viewed as a game, infers retaining the application of the cards from a deck. This may not appear to be helpful. You should remember as much as possible.

Both capacity and review are improved by making such connections. Another game that causes individuals to enhance memory and study is named narrating. Individuals must take every one of the thoughts that must be learned and fuse them in a story. Along these lines, they can review simpler which component trails another. The following technique infers virtual pictures that are joined to every one of the elements of a rundown. Recollecting an image, a smell, a taste, or a sound is more straightforward, so acknowledging such associations will help individuals to review a lot quicker.

Next, to improve memory and review, it is smarter to become familiar with the general thoughts before all else and the subtleties after. An outline is made like this. By recollecting the most significant parts, individuals can likewise review the nuances. Perusing books that are part down in general to detail way will help individuals to comprehend this idea. Furthermore, individuals are encouraged to examine resoundingly what they are realizing.

Joining more detects - hearing and seeing, in this specific case - encourages individuals to retain quicker. Talking about the subject of a book by utilizing own words appears likewise to be a system to improve memory and review. This technique decides individuals to arrange better and to check the exactness.

The most effective method to Improve Memory Skills - Best Tips to Improve Memory

The most effective method to improve memory abilities requires duty and not only can a fly by pill, but you also fly in your mouth. Your life would be simpler when you can hold and recover data as fast as a lightning and completion undertakings immediately as a result of it.

Sound propensities are mainly required to keep up great memory and to keep it fit as a fiddle.

Get enough rest

Rest is the thing that keeps our cerebrum working admirably. Perceive how we think and move quicker when we had enough rest the previous night? Rest additionally helps keep our recollections together.

Feed your brain

This doesn't just mean perusing books and adapting new things, however eating the right sorts of sustenance for the cerebrum. Pile up on pecans and different foods wealthy in omega-three like salmon and various fishes. Instructions to improve memory aptitudes includes eating steadily.

Watch and review

Focus on minor subtleties going on around you like whether the sales clerk who helped you wore a watch or some other frill. What shading was the vehicle before you on your way home? This may not be excessively, but rather it unquestionably hones our memory.

Mind exercise

Crossword riddles don't just ward off fatigue however practices your cerebrum as well. Another excellent exercise for your mind is a standard exercise routine. Just strolling for 30 minutes every day gives your mind and body the molding it needs.

Binaural beats

Regularly upgrade your memory by tuning in to binaural beats. Rather than consuming medications or drug that guarantees to improve your psychological handling, why not get your very own binaural beats mp3 which are not propensity shaping. You need a couple of minutes regularly as you hear them out like merely tuning in to music.

These tips are not the most critical thing in the world for memory improvement. There are more approaches to improve your memory; however, these are common and sure flame ways that you can undoubtedly do as such. Notwithstanding utilizing only one of these tips will, as of now represent a considerable advancement in your memory.

Fundamental Methods Of How To Improve Memory

There are many techniques that one can find out about when he needs to realize how to improve memory. By improving one's learning and recalling abilities, an individual can utilize the exercise that he has learned.

Relate the Information

There are many straightforward techniques you can pursue to improve memory. Educators utilize a portion of these strategies to instruct their understudies, so learning ends up more straightforward. The motivation behind learning a subject or exercise is lost if the understudy can't recall it. Subsequently, it is essential to realize how to improve memory so one can utilize the practice learned. Before acquiring a section, it is necessary to comprehend the motivation behind learning it.

Additionally, one should attempt to understand what the section is about. This will give the one learning a fundamental thought regarding the subject and set them up for the learning procedure. It is a smart thought to have an alarm mind when acquiring an important exercise consistently.

For successful memory the executives, one ought to learn troublesome points just when the brain is new and alert. More straightforward themes can be left for different occasions when the psyche is worn out. When the mind is new following a decent night's rest, it is in a superior position to get a handle on the scholarly material and can hold it well. This makes it simpler to review the academic data at the required time. To get it

Instructions to Improve Memory, it is a smart thought to pursue specific tips for learning troublesome subjects. Regularly the understudy needs to learn annoying statistical data points, which can't be recollected effectively. In such cases, it is a smart thought to relate the issue to be figured out how to some other point that the understudy thinks about. This will assist the understudy with connecting the data to some other material that he has officially adapted well. Thus, reviewing the data at the required time will be more straightforward.

A Healthy Lifestyle Is Essential

When learning another exercise, it is likewise valuable to discover some example in the material to be scholarly. For example, when adapting some new names, one can pursue some memory preparing strategies, learning the first letter of each title to shape another word. By recollecting the original word, one can get the clue, which will assist them with remembering each name.

To learn viable strategies for how to improve memory, it is additionally a smart thought to scribble down fundamental purposes of the part on a little bit of paper, which can be kept close nearby. During one's extra time, one can peruse through the composed material a few times, which will support maintenance and recall the content better. Notwithstanding these strategies, there are other fundamental focuses to make sure to enable the individuals to need to improve memory.

It is essential to pursue a decent way of life since it advances a stable personality. This requires a proper eating regimen and at any rate eight hours of rest, particularly after learning a troublesome or uninteresting point since maintenance is better when the brain is very still.

By utilizing basic techniques for how to improve memory, the understudy can appreciate the exercise and recall it well.

Chapter 18: The Feynman Technique

This very popular learning technique was devised by Nobel Peace Prize-winning physicist Richard Feynman as a means for him to make sure that he could understand things much more quickly and efficiently. The fact that he's not just a physicist – an already major mental accomplishment in and by itself – but an award-winning one is the only validation necessary for his acclaimed learning technique.

The technique involves 3 major principles or steps: teaching a child, reviewing, and organization and summarizing. A fourth principle or step, which is totally optional (but highly recommended) is transmitting.   Let's take a look at each in more detail.

Teaching A Child

This step doesn't necessarily mean you really have a child to teach the thing you want to learn, though that would be ideal. The point behind this is to be able to cut through all the fluff and go straight to the gist of the learning material or topic itself so that you can learn the topic, including all the necessary fluff. The assumption is this: if you can't teach it to an 8-year old, you don't really grasp the material.

Start by writing the topic or subject you want or need to learn at the top of a blank sheet of paper. Then below that, write everything you know about that topic or subject as if you will have to teach it to a child who can understand and focus enough attention to the basic ideas and principles you'll be explaining to him or her. Doing so will help you think about the topic in simpler and easier terms, which will allow you to learn the topic faster. Remember that simplicity always gets the job done!

Jotting down your ideas all throughout in a language that's simple enough for an 8-year old kid to understand forces you to really understand a topic or subject at a deepest and most basic levels, which will also allow you to simplify and understand the connections and relationships between the key points and ideas of the topic. If for some reason you're struggling at certain areas when jotting down these ideas, it simply means those are areas that you still don't understand well enough to express in the simplest of terms. Think of this as excellent opportunity to learn more and fortify your knowledge instead of perceiving it as shortcomings.

Reviewing

As mentioned earlier, there will be times you may face some knowledge gaps when learning or studying a topic or subject, i.e., areas where you struggle in jotting down the ideas in simple enough terms. It may be that you have a very hard time connecting important principles or concepts, forget something important, or simply find it very hard to explain them.

These are simply opportunities to make improvements on your understanding or learning of a particular topic or subject. These instances are actually signs that you've reached the current edge of your learning or understanding of the topic or subject. And guess what? True competence is knowing your learning ability's limits so that you can work on expanding those limits. This is where true learning starts!

By identifying your sticking points for a particular topic or subject, you get a reference point for going back to review your learning material and learn it again until you're able to explain those identified sticking points in a way that's simple enough for child to understand. When you go through the material again, you can focus more on those areas where your sticking points are located.

Organization and Simplification

After you have finished writing down your notes so that an 8-year old kid can understand the topic or subject of your learning materials, it's time to organize your notes in a way that the ideas and main points flow naturally and logically. You also have to make sure you don't include any technical jargon (emphasis on simplification) from your learning material – remember that the point of this technique is to be able to teach it at the most basic level of understanding.

Once you're done organizing and simplifying the language, read it aloud to yourself, carefully listen to any complicated or confusing words or statements. Those are good signs that you still need to work on your learning or understanding on certain areas of the material.

Transmission

This optional last step or principle is a rather fun one. Here, you will actually explain your learning material's main ideas and points to a kid or someone who has no clue about the topic. This is the real test of your application. If the child or person is able to clearly understand what you're saying, it means you have succeeded in learning the topic well enough to explain in in the simplest possible terms. However, if all you see are dazed looks of confusion, it may mean you need to hit the books a couple more times.

Chapter 19: What Is The Fastest Way To Learn French

Learning a new foreign language, especially in adulthood, can be a real challenge. It is necessary to have plenty of time to study, and when you learn the basics, you will need to constantly upgrade your vocabulary and learn the grammatical and syntactical rules.

It has been known that the easiest and fastest way to succeed at it is to visit the country of the language you want to learn, stay there for a while, listening and absorbing new words and knowledge. So, the first thing you should do is travel to France and spend some time there.

1. Use your free time to watch French movies

Although most of the time you be looking for a better job or working on other skills, you must understand that breaks are necessary as well.

2. Discover new music

We all know what it feels like when we had been upset and stressed and then suddenly we hear the sounds of some of our favorite songs on a radio station, in a coffee shop or in the car that just passed by us. It immediately helps us feel better.

Go to the MTV's website of the country whose language you are learning – MTV.fr and try to find the names of the most popular French singers. Then you can find their songs on YouTube and listen to them. Although at first you will hardly understand anything, you will feel the rhythm, the sound and energy of the French language.

3. Chat with native French speakers

Use chat websites and find people with whom you can chat. Find someone who has a French mother for example and wants to learn English. Then once you get to know each other you can start using Skype or similar programs for better communication.

4. Try some French recipes

Find recipes on the internet and try to cook some of the most characteristic dishes. That way you can learn many things related to food that everyone should know and more to get closer to the people whose language you are learning. This is one of the most effective ways to get more familiar with the French culture. And be sure that you will love it.

Maybe you will not become an expert on languages in a very short time, but these tips will certainly be able to help you if you decide to learn a foreign language without professional help.

Accelerated Learning of Italian

Accelerated Learning

Accelerated learning is a way to learn that involves learning at a quicker pace than ever before. Throughout the timeline of humanity, evolution has been slow because we have learnt things at a slow pace, which shows through the amount of technological progress we've had over thousands of years. The first remnants of accelerated learning were created in 1970, and since then we have progressed more so within a century than we had in thousands upon thousands of years.

If you look at the first computer, it was massive and only worked with megabits. Nowadays, because of accelerated learning, we have micro-chips that can store millions of megabits. This shows how much our world has evolved in such a short space of time. One thing that we have been able to learn quickly is languages. In particular, Italian.

The Italian Languages

I have visited Italy, and I can assure you that the language is beautiful. It is considered one of the easiest languages to learn in a short amount of time, which is why accelerated learning is so perfect if you are wanting to learn Italian quickly and efficiently. One thing about the Italian language is that you can truly feel them speak. They speak with their entire bodies. This makes learning the language easier because you're committing more of yourself to learning this information, which means that your mind will have an easier time remembering things about the language.

Italian and Accelerated Learning

Accelerated learning is done best when you have a great working environment and your senses are exposed to the language. The Italian language is such a passionate language. You walk around Rome, you will see people talking with their hands and bodies before you see them moving their mouths. Perhaps this is why the average person can learn to speak Italian confidently at around thirty weeks. You feel the language, as well as hear and speak it.

Something that is essential to know about accelerated learning is that it takes an extremely hard working person to pull it off. Hard work is what accelerated learning is built upon. You need to manage your time effectively, as well as be efficiently with your mind power. It is incredibly draining to learn something in such a small amount of time, but if you plan and put in the work, then accelerated learning will do wonders for you with a doubt.

Chapter 20: The Pomodoro Technique -

How to Ignore Distractions to Better

Manage Your Study Time

What can a tomato teach us about time management? A lot, if you are using a tomato-shaped kitchen timer to help you study. The Pomodoro Technique is an internationally used method of keeping time and increasing productivity. It was developed by a college student named Francesco Cirillo in the late 1980s, and he named his technique for the timer he used while working in his dormitory, which was shaped like a pomodoro tomato.

It's Pretty Simple...and Pretty Effective

There are only a handful of steps to the Pomodoro Technique:

1- Choose a task

2- Set a timer for 25 minutes

3- Work, uninterrupted, until the timer sounds

4- Make a checkmark on a piece of paper (one 'pomodoro' cycle)

5- Take a 3-5 minute break

6- Repeat until you've got four pomodoro checkmarks

7- Take a 15-30 minute break, and start over

Proponents of the method say it improves productivity by reducing distractions. Life, of course, has a way of interrupting, especially in this digital age of instant communication. The Pomodoro Technique will help you handle distractions by prioritizing tasks and setting boundaries.

Broken Pomodoros

If you come up against a distraction, there are two ways to handle it. If there is an incoming call or email that simply cannot wait, end your pomodoro timer prematurely (no checkmark!) and attend to the interruption. Then when you're ready, reset the timer and try again.

If at all possible, try to tell the person interrupting you that you will get back to them in a little while and continue your current pomodoro cycle. Doing so will set a boundary with your colleagues or friends, showing that your work or study is important to you, but that you are not uncaring of their inquiries. A simple "I'll get back to you in a few" should suffice, but be sure to follow through on that promise. You don't want to sacrifice good communication, either.

Why Does It Work?

Giving yourself a task and a set period of time to complete it makes you focus, but because the time period is a manageable

25 minutes, it doesn't seem unconquerable or overextended. There's also that good old competition factor- can you beat the clock and complete your task? Can you resist the urge to look at your phone or your email?

The break portion of the pomodoro cycle is important, too. It gives you a moment to breathe and to reset your brain. Even if you didn't complete the first task, you can give yourself a checkmark for working uninterrupted and jump back in when it's time to restart the clock.

This time management method appeals to our human need to feel accomplished, teaches us about the time needed to perform certain tasks, and imparts the skill of working with the clock, not against it. When you've trained your brain to realize you **can** achieve tasks in a set timeframe, you'll eventually be able to determine how long a task will take **before** you begin. That knowledge will boost your productivity in study and your credibility at work.

Does It Work for Everyone?

The Pomodoro Technique is an easy-to-follow time management method, and has proven to be quite effective since its introduction. However, not all methods are right for every person. Critics of the system say the 25-minute timer can actually interrupt workflow and make it more difficult to complete tasks.

Other people think the system is too rigid, or have a hard time using it every day because of meetings or other obligations. The creator himself, Francesco Cirillo, says the time periods can be adjusted if necessary, but that 25 minutes just seems to be the sweet spot. Like any method of time management, it's up to you to give it a try and determine if it's right for you.

Now that we've gone over study and practice habits, delved into time management, talked about learning myths, and dug into the physiology of memory and brain function, let's look at some very specific learning methods to help you achieve your learning goals. Part II of this book is full of tips and techniques, with plenty of embedded exercises to get

187

you and your brain in gear and on the path
to new skills.

CHAPTER 21: WHY DO YOU WANT THIS JOB?

This question also seems like a throw away but it is a question very often asked in an interview. Of course the main reason anyone wants any job is for money but the employer is searching for your true interest level. Just as in the previous chapter the employer would like to find someone who is truly invested in the line of work for which they are interviewing. Someone who is passionate is more likely to remain in the position longer and will take the job more seriously. Those who have a personal passion are more likely to bring about positive change and work ethic and these are things an employer will see as an asset.

When asked this question begin your response with how and where you found the position. What about the job first snagged your attention and made you decide it was a job you had to apply for?

189

Refer to specific wording in the job listing which stood out to you or aspects of the job which made you feel you would be a good fit with elongated interest in investing your time in working with the company.

After you have begun your answer this way you can ask questions you already know the answers to and explain then how those answers fit into your personal goals and passions for the position. Within those responses you can then explain how those answers make the job even more interesting and rewarding to you in your job, and if possible, your personal life as well.

Focus your response in explaining how the job matches what you are looking for as a career path and the growth within that path. Specify that you are drawn to the mission of the company and believe in the same core values such as X,Y,Z. You will want to do your research and find out the core values of the company and find ones which match your own personal beliefs. Explaining that you feel you can provide a lot of value to the company due to your experience and expertise and are looking forward to all you can learn from the position and are excited to undergo the growth process.

You can also talk about how you are strongly motivated by the core values of the company and strive for similar points not only in your career but your personal life outside of work. When discussing the details, you can emphasis the portions of the work you would be excited to perform and how you are drawn to that type of work with excitement and purpose. When companies know the person they have hired is fulfilling a life's purpose they feel they have hired someone who will be a longstanding asset to the company.

Furthermore, you can mention how you think you would be a great fit for the role because of what you have learned about the company. If you feel you are a natural fit for the role in question and that the job does not only fulfill needs for the company but needs for you as an employee. The desire to be a willing participant and contributor to the forward motion of the company will be a deciding factor in who the company decides to hire in the role.

Having done your research on the company and knowing what the company is known for, the industry it supports, where the company is based, and how many employees the company has, will help you in your discussion. Statements which vocalize that the company is an attractive place for people with your skills and talents to work because of the companies ability to utilize their employees skills and talents for the betterment of the business will help you show your deep ties to the type of work for which you are applying.

Within your response avoid saying negative things about previous positions, companies, or employees. Someone who is willing to be negative in a job interview is likely to be negative on the job and will bring with them negativity which can rub off on other employees. Potential employers are looking for people who will uplift moral and not bring it down.

Furthermore, avoid speaking about previous positions as being too easy or too difficult. Anything which can make your previous positions seem trivial, or as a burden, will ultimately label you as someone who is not fully invested in the job and has a more self centered attitude. It is better to focus your energy on ensuring you show you take the job at hand very seriously.

WHAT ARE YOUR INTERESTS?

Employers are always wanting employees who have a well-rounded skill set and experience background. Some positions focus on some factors which may be more desirable to an employee than others or some companies may have a separate position for those aspects completely. When asked this question the employer is once again checking to see how much the position will really hold your interest. They ask these types of questions to weed out potential employees who would be more satisfied with positions which are better suited for skills and experience which holds their interest.

When answering this question you should focus on what initially drove you to this type of work. What first sparked your interest in the field of study or work gaining experience? Was there something in your life which made the type of work extremely rewarding or perhaps there is a life's passion and need to be in a job which allows you certain intrinsic rewards the position provides? Focus on how the job you desire is the position for which you have been working towards and would love nothing more than to help the company succeed.

When answering these types of questions it is always beneficial to respond in ways which show a group centered mentality. The purpose of you being hired is to help the overall success of the company and the mission not for your own personal financial gain. Group centered mentalities demonstrate a work ethic which is less likely to make self centered decisions and ultimately will be the best for a company. Those who work more for their own gain are less likely able to work well in groups and follow instructions.

Avoid telling long stories or going off on tangents when responding. Keep your answers precise and to the point. Keeping answers short and simple will also keep the attention of your interviewer and keep their interest longer. It will also demonstrate an ability to keep information detailed but concise.

WHAT ARE YOUR STRENGTHS IN A TEAM?

Employers who are asking this question are doing so because their employees will often be expected to work as a team. Many companies today are set up for success by working in small groups and even viewing the entire company as one large team. If an employee is unable to work well in a team mentality they may not be best suited for this type of company set up.

When responding it is best to focus on what attributes and skills you can provide which can help a team set up and have helped in the past. Talk specifically about a time when you had worked in a team

195

before and what your specific roll was within that team. Stating specifics will aid you in being detailed without taking too much time and will also allow your employer know you have actually worked within a team.

Being specific enough to detail which exact position and whom the supervisor was will allow your potential employer to make contact with whomever was involved should they desire more details. It is also a good idea to remain as positive as possible, give praise to other members of the team, and specify how each of your contributions was helpful when using them together. This shows your potential employer that you give credit where credit is due and do not see yourself as the only contributor in a group setting.

Even if your experience was that you pulled all of the weight, it is better to always provide a positive attitude towards any situation. Chose your wording carefully and be kind towards those who were assigned to the team. Talk about what you enjoyed about working with a team and how it helped you grow.

When talking about your strengths state the things you are proud of and what you have worked on. You can also go into a little detail on how you have worked to become better in the areas you now consider a strength. Focus on your goals and how your strengths are helping you gain your footing to get closer to achieving them. You can also discuss what strengths you have which help in a team which may have been learned or strengthened on the job or through the mentorship of another employee or supervisor. Explaining what things motivate you to work hard within a group is also helpful.

Avoid speaking negatively about a project, the group, a particular person, or the company in question. Once again this will only alert your potential employer to the possibility of you being a negative influence. It is always better to remain positive and speak kindly about every situation, even those which may have been less than optimal.

Also avoid speaking as though you were the only contributor in a group. Even if this were true a potential employer could take this as a sign of being self-centered. Employers like to work with those who are willing and able to work in a group setting. People who spend their time talking about the lack of ability from those in their team will likely be ones who are quick to complain and cause friction within a group.

Instead of talking about what aspects of the group setting were poor, or explaining why you would work better alone, do your best to talk about how working in a group ultimately helps move the entire team of the all encompassing company forward towards its goals. You may also speak towards the exemplary abilities of each person bringing their talents to the team. Doing this will show you are humble in your own abilities as well and that you are willing to give energy and effort towards another person's success.

When potential employees show they are willing to put their own personal goals aside to help a team member, or the team as a whole, shine brightly, the potential employer will see this not as a sign of weakness but as a sign that you are a true team player. The overall success matters more than the gold star attached to your personal name. Companies like to see people who are not out for their own fame and glory.

Conclusion

If you are looking to improve your grades or simply have a better performance in translating the knowledge acquired through the study, it is always possible to appeal to some techniques and habits that can be implemented during this task and that will make studying easier and effective .

Just as there are techniques for improving memory , simple techniques can also improve performance in the study, although of course some will find it easier to study certain subjects and others will be more difficult or boring.

1. Define a comfortable and supportive study space

The **study space** should lack any kind of distraction, but also be very monotonous and boring. Ideally a public place but quiet, such as a library or even an outdoor park. If it is in your home, you should avoid places where there are distractions like a telephone, television or the presence of other people. A computer with Internet access is a double-edged sword: it can be a great source of distraction but you can also find interesting material, it is convenient to use it only for punctual information.

2. Clearly define your program of study

First of all you must be focused on each of the things you study, therefore, it is not advisable to wander through different subjects or exercises, which cover much of what you should study, but without focusing on any of them really . A well-defined and orderly program will help to clearly mark where you should focus. What's more, you can even organize a schedule in which you plan every day what topics you study, in this way you will ensure that by fulfilling this schedule you will cover the entire program for the day of your exam.

3. Try to interpret what the teachers want

If you attend classes regularly and pay attention, you will have a good idea about what would be the best way to meet the demands imposed on a test as much as possible to the expectations of the teacher. It is also important to note to the teachers that you are interested in the class you are taking.

4. Learn to separate the important from the accessory

All the books that you will have to face when studying will surely be divided into chapters, well defined and titled and the first thing to remember are those titles, as they will give a global, orderly and divided view of the main themes and concepts.

Similarly, many books include at the end of each chapter a section of questions that allows (or does not) affirm whether the main concepts of each section have been understood. Paying attention to these tools is easier and more beneficial.

5. Define an orderly and healthy routine

Many times in the middle of a period of study you end up completely altering the usual routine, wasting time, eating, sleeping and studying at any time. It is advisable to have a clear timetable for the study, to define the goals that you want to reach in each study interval, and then to have a good rest and a healthy diet, propitious to maintain the energies And attention well placed in the study material.

In addition, keep in mind that to retain and understand any type of material is necessary to read and review several times (at least three), so that this is part of your permanent memory.

www.ingramcontent.com/pod-product-compliance
Lightning Source LLC
Chambersburg PA
CBHW060320030426
42336CB00011B/1131